Praise for *Dream Big and Win*

"Every entrepreneur and business leader needs to place *Dream Big and Win* at the top of their reading list. As the sales coach for Liz Elting, I was there at the beginning, an up-close witness to the phenomenal growth of her business to a billion dollars. Her story is a master class in building a profitable hypergrowth business. Read it and reap!"

—Jack Daly,
CEO coach and bestselling author

"Elting's battle cry is that if she can do it, you can do it, too. Then she takes it one step further by detailing the actions required to take an idea from a dorm room to a boardroom, with insights on everything the leader or entrepreneur needs to know, from sales to corporate culture. A must-read for anyone who wants to build their dream."

—Gretchen Carlson,
journalist, co-founder Lift Our Voices, bestselling author and
female-empowerment advocate

"An inspiring account of a successful philanthropist's journey from being the only woman in the room to sitting at the head of the table and breaking barriers for other women to do the same."

—Scott Galloway,
professor of Marketing, NYU Stern School of Business,
and bestselling author of *Adrift*

"Grit, passion, and sweat equity took Liz Elting from the dorm room to the boardroom. Now she is doing what true leaders do—showing other women how to follow in her path."

—Tina Brown,
award-winning editor and bestselling author

"All entrepreneurs win big and learn from Liz Elting's highly successful startup journey. Sacrifice. Decisions. Anguish. Risk. Reward. It's all here. Every entrepreneur will find takeaways on every page and learn from her experience and mistakes—all of which she lays bare for you to read. An amazing, fast-paced tale."

—**Danny Briere,**
prolific author, inventor, entrepreneur,
investor, and ecosystem builder

"It's impossible to read Elting's *Dream Big and Win* and not be inspired. From instructions on creating a positive corporate culture to figuring out the problem the marketplace needs you to solve, this book is a prescriptive guide to building an empire and creating your dream life."

—**Joanne Berger-Sweeney,**
president, Trinity College

"Elting presents a superbly organized blend of principles and tools for forging one's own path in the business world, brought to life with sharp examples from the corporate world, many from her own extraordinary entrepreneurial journey. I dare you to read this and not be inspired."

—**Raghu Sundaram,**
dean, NYU Stern School of Business

Dream BIG and WIN

Translating Passion into Purpose and Creating a Billion-Dollar Business

LIZ ELTING

WILEY

Published by John Wiley & Sons, Inc., Hoboken, New Jersey.
Published simultaneously in Canada.

For general information on our other products and services or for technical support, please
contact our Customer Care Department within the United States at (800) 762-2974, outside
the United States at (317) 572-3993 or fax (317) 572-4002.

Wiley also publishes its books in a variety of electronic formats. Some content that appears in
print may not be available in electronic formats. For more information about Wiley products,
visit our web site at www.wiley.com.

Library of Congress Cataloging-in-Publication Data is Available:

ISBN 9781119904366 (Cloth)
ISBN 9781119904373 (ePub)
ISBN 9781119904380 (ePDF)

Cover Design: Paul Mccarthy
Cover Image: © Getty Images | XVISION
Back Cover Author Image: © Melanie Dunea

SKY10052225_072823

For my husband, Mike, for your unwavering support and dedication.

Our love has indeed been a wild ride!

For my proudest achievements, Zack and Jay.

I can't wait to see the good you both put forth in this world.

For my parents, Judy and Everett.

Thank you for shaping me into the person I am today and for teaching me how to turn my passions into my purpose.

I love you all so very much.

"If you don't have integrity, you have nothing. You can't buy it. You can have all the money in the world. But if you are not a moral and ethical person, you really have nothing."

—Henry Kravis

"I do not know anyone who has got to the top without hard work. That is the recipe. It will not always get you to the top but should get you pretty near."

—Margaret Thatcher

"If you don't encounter setbacks in your career, if you don't have doubts and disappointments, let me tell you, you're not dreaming big enough."

—Michael Bloomberg

"All our dreams can come true if we have the courage to pursue them."

—Walt Disney

Contents

Introduction

The unspoken truth about succeeding in business—or life, for that matter—is that hopes and dreams on their own are not enough to create success. Of course, passion is a must, but you need more than that. Having a mantra can be a powerfully motivating touchstone, but amorphous concepts like "manifesting" or "believing" will get a person only so far. Constructing a vision board is a fine way to imagine where one might be in 10 years. The problem is that cutting and pasting and opening tubes of glitter have nothing to do with the steps needed to realize that tangible representation of the life you've depicted on that poster board. (Also, you're never going to get all that glitter out of your carpet.)

So I wrote this book as a guide not only for how to dream big, but also how to win.

I learned that the surest way to satisfy my desire for success was to act. TransPerfect, the billion-dollar language solutions company that began as a dream in an NYU dorm room, required me to employ something more than a mantra; I needed verbs.

Why verbs? Because verbs are *actions*.

Verbs are the beating heart of a sentence and they're the most fundamental element of language. The written word can't exist without them. Verbs create a mutual understanding by delivering the same meaning to all involved in the conversation. That's why verbs are among the first words students use when learning to communicate in foreign languages. For example, French teachers start conjugating *avoir* (to have) and *être* (to be) right after the lesson on saying *bonjour* (howdy). Sure, the ability to greet others in their language is nice, but that Parisian sidewalk café waiter is never going to bring you a croissant if you can't ask for one.

Verbs are fundamental for dreams because action is fundamental to success. (Full disclosure: I wouldn't have been so intent on founding the world's largest language solutions company if I weren't a bit of a language nerd.)

So you'll find each chapter in this book organized around a verb form (technically, a gerund). Every chapter will highlight a different action for you to take in the pursuit of turning your leadership dreams into reality. I draw from my experience as an entrepreneur, *Forbes* contributor, philanthropist, and working mother. I'll share tales of my successes and, just as important, I'll dissect my failures. (Crash and burn? Definitely not my favorite verbs.) I'll relate this advice using my philosophy, as well as anecdotes from my own career and personal life, because context is key.

This isn't just a business book; rather, it's a candid look at how I built the company that landed me on the *Forbes* list of richest self-made women. I'll also feature facts, figures, and quotes from other successful businesspeople on each topic because any good leader knows it's not all about her.

In the beginning, back when I shared the NYU dorm room with a cat named Marbella (Molly for short), a boyfriend and business partner named Phil, a home-use printer, and more cockroaches than I care to recall, I used to tell myself that I'd work today like no one else would, so I could live tomorrow like no one else could.

However, this mantra was more than the preface to my hopes because I paired it with verbs. My mantra of dreaming big and winning, when fortified with actions such as setting goals and holding myself accountable, became a plan of attack.

Yours can, too.

Beginning to Dream

1

Creating

On a sweltering morning in August of 1992, I was living in New York City, fresh out of grad school. The entire city seemed miserable that day, as the mercury surged upwards, hitting 90-plus degrees before 8 a.m. Everyone was surly, damp, and unhappy, save for me.

As I strolled up Park Avenue South, I violated all the rules I'd learned in the past five years living in Manhattan. I smiled. I nodded. I made eye contact with each passerby. I even committed the cardinal sin of saying hello. People rushed past me, assuming the heat had driven me out of my mind. What strangers on the street didn't know was that my joy stemmed from finally having landed a job.

The country was still recovering from a recession at that time. I'd quickly learned that a grad school degree was no guarantee of success, no promise of gainful employment. I'd interviewed for months and had been in a full-on panic as late spring turned to midsummer. My mailbox was full of ding letters. I papered the walls of my studio apartment with rejections from places like Goldman Sachs and J.P. Morgan. I was miserable. Until then, I never knew how many ways a letter could say, "Thanks, but no thanks," or how a single sheet of paper could alter my destiny.

The idea of not working was entirely foreign to me. I'd maintained some form of employment since I was 10 years old and had hustled to find neighborhood grade-schoolers I could escort to the door of their classrooms for a small fee. While my parents were emotionally supportive, they made it clear that as an adult with an advanced degree, I was fiscally responsible for myself.

Early on, their lesson was that no one would ever need to rescue me if I learned how to save myself. Still, I was grateful.

To economize, Phil, my boyfriend at the time, and I downgraded our living situation. We moved from a Tudor City studio apartment to NYU housing as he was finishing his last year there. The irony was not lost on me that my big prize for graduating with an MBA from NYU's Leonard N. Stern School of Business was moving *into* an NYU dorm room. Still, we were grateful to land at Washington Square Village. With some creative accounting, we could delay rent payments through the fall semester, possibly even until the end of the school year.

Liz's Life Lesson

Never underestimate the acumen of a broke MBA. They are scrappy, they are resourceful, they are hungry, and they are willing to work 100-plus hours a week to figure out how to spin hay into gold.

Washington Square Village, identifiable by its Soviet-era-chic cinderblocks of dingy white bricks turned gray, had been built in the 1950s. The facility had not been upgraded, maintained, or cleaned in any way since then. Decades of housing students had taken its toll. Everything was worn and depressing. Fortunately, we had our own private (rust-stained, linoleum-chipped, microscopic) bathroom; that may have been the dorm room's only redeeming quality.

Yet none of that mattered as I made my way north because *this was my first day of work*! I'd been hired by Paresco, the proprietary trading division of a major French bank. I was finally employed, thank God.

I didn't want to spare the cash for a subway token, so I walked the 30 blocks from 2 Washington Square Village to my new office at 24th and Park. Visible heat waves rose from the sidewalk in front of me, creating a mirage effect. As I hustled up Park, sweat rolled down my back. I felt my blouse sticking to my skin, so I took off my fuchsia silk suit jacket.

I've always been the most corporate-dressed of all my coworkers my entire career; that's just how I've done it. Years earlier, while I was working at a dry cleaners in high school, an immaculately clad professional woman had told me to always dress for the job you wanted, not the job you had. Her wardrobe was made up of finely woven wools, delicate silks, and airy linens, everything luxurious and meticulously crafted with wrapped seams. I was so enamored of her wardrobe that her advice stuck with me; I pledged that someday I'd make enough money to buy beautiful clothes, too. While throwing on jeans or a pair of Golden Goose sneakers might be easier in the workplace today, it's just not my style.

My only nod to comfort that day was my commuter footwear. I didn't want to hoof it 30 blocks in my pumps. Like Tess McGill in the classic '80s women's empowerment movie *Working Girl*, I donned an old pair of tennis shoes. (FYI, I've since figured out the whole wearing cute flats and swapping them out thing.)

While I was excited to start my new career, I swallowed my disappointment not to be back at Euramerica, at the time, the world's largest translation company, with about 90 employees. I'd held that job prior to attending grad school. I adored the work there, every aspect of it, from working with talented linguists to solving clients' problems. But my work there was bigger than the day-to-day tasks; my role had a purpose that impacted the greater good. I loved the feeling of doing a job that made a difference, of being an agent for change, in some small part. I was impressed with Euramerica's mission of helping entities better understand each other through shared language. If the world was ever going to come together and learn to appreciate different cultures, it would be because we were all *found* in translation.

The Euramerica staff included many 20-somethings. They were my second family and entire social circle in a city where I knew almost no one. Plus, the job was so much fun and so exciting that it never felt like work. My father had many philosophies on careers, dovetailing around the concept that if you pursue what you love, it will always work out. He used to say that it's only work if you'd rather be doing something else, and there was nothing else I'd rather have been doing. I'd spent my life to that point learning and embracing foreign languages, having traveled and lived abroad. A future in translation services made sense in my heart.

In my head? Not so much.

The lure of a nice paycheck was too powerful; financial independence was so important to me. I wanted the freedom to choose, to play by my own rules. My parents reinforced these lessons ever since I can remember, so I knew that earning my own living meant I never had to rely on or be beholden to anyone but myself.

So I'd left my beloved employ at Euramerica to attend Stern only because there had been no clear path to advancement or higher earnings and it seemed like the prudent course to pursue. (The late 1980s and early 1990s were a time in America where society idolized the Gordon Gekkos of the business world and embraced the notion that "greed is good." This gave rise to packs of Wolves of Wall Street.

No one ever explained or apologized for the desire to create wealth back then.)

Just the Facts

Female MBA grads still make an average of $11,000 less than their male counterparts after graduation in commensurate positions, and more than $60,000 less after a decade.[1]

While I longed for money in the bank, it was about more than a balance sheet for me. I was driven toward financial success as an acknowledgment of the effort I'd put forth. I didn't want money to prove my worth to anyone else; I wanted it because it would be a tangible representation to me of my best self. For those reasons, I'd sublimated what I wanted and sought work in international finance, instead of what I considered the more dynamic field of language translation.

I'd been born into a family where creativity had always been at the forefront of who we were, from my mom making homemade party favors to my dad composing our own family theme song. My father worked in marketing and advertising and had been the mind behind some of the most iconic campaigns for General Foods, Chesebrough-Ponds (now Unilever), and Procter & Gamble. My mother was equally brilliant and talented, penning plays and writing music to incorporate into her career as an educator. My folks weren't so big on giving us material items; instead, they were all about providing experiences. My father even moved us to Portugal for a time when I was in grade school so he could open a Kentucky Fried Chicken franchise (not kidding— and more on this later). Their parenting style favored creativity and independence, as they encouraged my sister and me to find ways to work out our differences on our own, rather than having them resolve our problems for us. They were my greatest teachers and mentors. My parents set the groundwork for me to always seek out those who inspire me. No matter where you are in your professional (or personal) development, there's always someone out there who can motivate you to do more and be more; you just must be open to finding them.

Given my background and interests, I'd likely have been better suited for the more right-brained marketing track at Stern. Instead, I majored in finance along with international business, thinking that's what I *should* do with my life. I'd not yet come to appreciate my father's advice that when you do what you love, the money will follow.

The Beginning of the Beginning

When I arrived at my new office that morning, I quickly freshened up and changed into my heels. This was it—the big dance. I was hired in the international finance field, specifically to do equity arbitrage. Arbitrage funds capitalize on the mispricing between the cash and futures market. James, the man who'd be my new boss, summed up the concept by saying, "Essentially, we exploit the differences in pricing of identical assets and then make a lot more money."

"Is that ethical?" I had asked.

"It's not unethical," he'd assured me, which *definitely* didn't sound like Orwellian doublespeak. "It's just a trading technique."

While aspects of my new job were foreign to me—and not particularly riveting—generating revenue was why I went to B-school. I was still intent on changing the world, but I thought I'd have a better shot at it if I had more financial means. Plus, I liked the idea of learning the ins and outs of international finance. Because it was a French bank, that seemed like a nod to my passion for languages, which had been my major in undergrad. Did I have a burning desire to be a proprietary trader? No. But I'd do it until I was solvent enough to figure out what I was meant to do next. Sometimes on your professional journey, you may temporarily find yourself in the wrong place, but keep in mind that it can be a stepping stone, and any experience can be valuable.

That first morning, James detailed the job's specifics, walking me through how we invested money to make more money. Then he said, "The way it works as far as vacation days, as far as lunch, is we have no specific time set aside; we have no set number of days off. These are big boy rules. We work, and when we need a break, we take a break."

At the time, those rules sounded great—so grown up and progressive! But now I know this translates to "You'll never get a break, go to lunch, or take a vacation." (Trust me on this.)

Liz's Life Lesson

If it sounds too good to be true, it probably is. No one gives you something for nothing. Do your due diligence, conduct your research, and ask around to make sure you're getting the full story.

James escorted me to my new desk. The first thing I noticed was that I was the only woman in the room. That was surprising. My grad school classes at NYU were about 40 percent female, so I anticipated the workforce having a similar composition. I briefly wondered where all the ladies were, and then I remembered that most of my girlfriends at NYU majored in marketing, not finance. While marketing seemed more interesting, I assumed I'd make less money. I felt I had to try finance. Seventy percent of Stern grads at the time majored in finance, and Paresco was the best job offer I'd received.

It turns out that not only was I the first woman these guys had ever worked with, judging from their behavior, it's possible I was the first woman *they'd ever met*. Our office was enveloped in a dense fog of testosterone, hair gel, and Drakkar Noir. So much swearing. So much shouting.

I'd looked forward to the job for many reasons, one of them being the camaraderie I'd previously found at Euramerica. That office had been so social, and our work and personal lives had become enmeshed. We all experienced what it was like to be an idealistic young professional in New York together. I loved being around other people who shared my "work hard/play hard" philosophy. We'd go from our grueling yet rewarding day helping our international clients out to parties or comedy clubs together. Everything was an exciting new experience with my coworkers.

However, Paresco turned out to be far less of a fun and welcoming melting pot and more of a fraternity house where I'd not been granted membership. As the f-bombs detonated all around me, as the conversation turned to the grittier details of recent sexual exploits, and as the chatter eventually focused on how much the Mets sucked, I thought, *This might not be where I make my good friends*. My first day at

Paresco began at 8 a.m. and ended at midnight. This was the norm, and I could absolutely live with the schedule. I mean, on my first day at Euramerica, I'd ended up staying until 2 a.m. because I was seeing my first project through to completion. I left in the wee hours of the morning feeling so exhilarated that I could barely sleep. I'd hoped to find the same at Paresco, but I quickly discovered that I wasn't in love with the position itself. I didn't anticipate it being so . . . dry. The entirety of my job entailed putting numbers in a spreadsheet, then filling out a form and faxing it to a bank, then getting back a different form and starting the entire process again, lather, rinse, repeat for 12 to 16 hours a day.

My coworkers didn't make the long hours more pleasant either. While we all held the same position, there was a distinct divide between them and me, one that became more pronounced every day. Many came from old-money families and had attended Ivy League universities. The ones without the pedigrees were connected by having been blue blood–adjacent through athletics or memberships in fraternities and social clubs.

The guys in the office would return Monday mornings with sunburnt foreheads and noses, having spent the weekends on the links or a boat or a friend's family compound in Southampton. (As for me, I'd sweated in front of a box fan in the bleak dorm room, reading books on arbitrage trading.) Many landed the job not because of skill but due to social or family connections. So it didn't sit well with them to see me hail from somewhere other than off the Social Register, yet hold my own.

Especially because I was a woman.

Here's the thing—I hailed from a sort of privilege, too. However, my privilege entailed 26 years of never being told that I couldn't achieve something because of my gender or race. Both of my parents set that example. My mother had an admirable work ethic; in fact, she only stopped working a few years ago at age 78. Her actions showed me there was no barrier to achievement. And she had done everything from teaching to counseling to winning Teacher of the Year. As for my dad, when he was president of the Canadian operation of Grey Advertising, he had 16 division leaders—and half of them were women. Sexism was never a consideration for him; he simply hired the best person for the job.

What Gender Gap?

You might assume I'd have encountered the gender gap in B-school, but it was a nonissue. I guess we'd all proved our worth simply by having been admitted. We were all competitive with each other. I never presumed I wasn't an equal, nor was I treated any differently. Grad school felt like a level playing field. I was blissfully ignorant of the concept of sexism. I didn't even join Stern's Women in Business group when I was at NYU. I recall thinking, *Why would I need that?*

Just the Facts

Per career coach Ashley Stahl in *Forbes*, "Studies have shown that the pay gap is perpetuated by the ask gap. Women typically do not ask for the same amount as men when negotiating salaries. On average, women ask for 6 percent less."[2]

As days passed, I noticed increasingly how I was viewed as inferior at the office, and not because of my performance. I could have navigated around that perception, proving them all wrong by excelling at the work I didn't enjoy.

Instead, my coworkers considered me an assistant, not a peer, despite *having been hired for the same exact job*.

Let that sink in for a moment.

For example, we'd all be working on our assigned number-crunching and paper-pushing, and when the phone would ring, every one of them would shout, "Liz! Phone!!"

Somehow it was incumbent on me to fetch the phone because I wore a skirt to work.

I tried to be a pleaser back then, a team player, so I'd find myself going along and just answering the damn phone. On the outside, I smiled through my gritted teeth. On the inside, I fumed. I'd been hired as a junior trader, not a receptionist. I thought, *I can't even stand being here and now I have to get the phone for these jerks?* It was the worst. I swear I started to hear, "Liz! Phone!!" in my dreams. Or nightmares.

Every morning when I laced up my Keds for the sweltering hike to the office, I felt an impending sense of dread. I got to the point that just seeing the shoes sitting by the front door would trigger me. I was miserable all the time. I'd placate myself by recounting my accomplishments at Euramerica, like being 22 years old and managing and motivating my own staff. I'd remind myself of the time I'd written out my case for why I deserved a 30 percent raise—and received it, based on the caliber of my argument. Or all those instances of using my creativity to deliver the best service for my clients.

Despite how much I loved being there, Euramerica hadn't been a perfect organization. In fact, I was often frustrated by its limited deliverables and lengthy turnaround times. Euramerica had the potential to be so much better, but the management resisted change. Still, I felt valued there, and I could see how my efforts made a difference, not just to my clients but in a greater societal context. We were facilitating communication that might have never previously existed. When I'd tell people what I did for a living back then, their eyes would light up, and they'd have a million questions. Language translation was exciting because I was working with linguists around the globe. Now, when I mentioned equity arbitrage, eyes would glaze over. I couldn't blame them; it bored me, too.

In simple economic terms, I couldn't afford to take the financial step back to work in translation services again. On the other hand, while I made good money at Paresco, I worried it was at the cost of becoming subservient to my colleagues. I resented how my job was invalidating the narrative I had for myself my whole life, that with enough effort, I could crush any goal I'd set.

Had I begun to accept the soft tyranny of their lowered expectations because I was a woman?

A few weeks into my tenure, in the throes of a stifling early September, I'd become quite adept at managing my tasks. I still didn't like the work, but I developed a proficiency. There will be times in your career when you feel penned in or underappreciated and you'll want to just phone it in. This concept has recently been dubbed "quiet quitting." I urge you to not give in to the temptation of not giving the job your all. **Circumstances are temporary, but your attitude is permanent. Quiet quitting sets an ugly precedent within yourself; don't succumb to it.**

I was determined to make the best of my situation, so I went in to talk to James about adding to my responsibilities. I brought a legal pad and ballpoint pen to take notes. I lived by the quote "Nothing in hand, nothing in head."

"I keep finishing my work early," I explained.

I suspect I finished more quickly because I didn't engage in the frat-boy antics all around me, such as recounting the movie *Wayne's World*, scene for scene. If someone asked me, "Asphinctersayswhat?" one more time, I could not be held responsible for my actions. (To this day, I'm mad at Mike Myers.) I continued, "I'm anxious to learn the business and I don't want any downtime, so I'm hoping there's something else I can do."

Maybe there was a hidden aspect of equity arbitrage I'd appreciate? Perhaps something client-facing? Or some problem-solving I could tackle, digging in and using my education and creativity? Surely James noticed my degree of motivation. He did hire me, after all. He wouldn't buy into the rising tide of sexism washing across the trading floor, pulling me under in its wake . . . right?

James pondered my request, thoughtfully scratching his chin, gold cufflinks glinting in his perfectly pressed French cuffs. His fingertips were neatly manicured, and his palms pink and smooth, clearly having never been used for physical labor. "I guess . . . " he began, gazing off to the trading floor. "I guess you could scan the storage closet and see what we need."

He nodded, as though agreeing with himself. "Then go around to all the guys and ask them if there are any office supplies they could use."

That's the moment when I realized from where the office's culture of inequality stemmed. Not only did I have my MBA, unlike many of the guys who'd joined the firm right after undergrad, but I also had three years of professional experience. Given those factors, James was still convinced the best use of my time was ordering printer toner and counting rolls of toilet paper. I should have had a Norma Rae moment right then and there. I should have jumped up on his desk and demanded equality.

I didn't.

I was too much of a pleaser to disagree, to state my case, to argue for the best use of my experience and education. I felt like my voice, the one that had been so clear and confident for most of my 26 years, had suddenly been silenced. I grabbed my notebook and exited his office.

I'm loath to admit it, but I may even have said, "Thank you."

I'd made a huge mistake in taking this job. Equity arbitrage was not for me. This had to be the reason there were so few women working on Wall Street or in finance at the time. I knew it wasn't because a woman couldn't do the job.

Instead, maybe it was because a woman wouldn't want to handle all the superfluous nonsense that went hand in hand with the job. I mean, how could she help bring her team to victory when the other players refused to acknowledge her team membership? How could she fight the preconceived notions that she didn't belong, regardless of empirical proof otherwise, if that was the entrenched, conventional wisdom?

Had finance been my passion, I'd have looked at this whole situation differently. But I realized I wanted to work with people more than with numbers. What excited me about Euramerica was how much I loved interacting with clients and translators, plus the opportunity to work with languages and global business. Given the choice, I wanted to work with people and words instead of spreadsheets and numbers.

I took a long look at myself. I was better than this. I deserved better than this. I couldn't be part of a company that didn't see the value of embracing and developing every one of its employees. So I needed to demand better than this.

Liz's Life Lesson

No one will value you if you don't first value yourself.

Of course, the phone began to ring at that moment. Of course it did. *"Liz! Phone!!"*

What else could I do? I answered it; the expectation was established. I realized the bar was already set so low for me that I'd never be able to limbo beneath it. After I completed the call, I went from desk to desk, querying my coworkers about their office supply needs.

I did my job. And I hated it.

I've always loved working; that's been a constant in my life since childhood. But for the first time in this situation, I couldn't muster the strength to push through it with a smile on my face. My heart wasn't in it. I despised the job—especially because there were too many strings attached to it. My fear was that Paresco wasn't a one-off, that no matter where I'd go in banking and finance, I'd encounter a similar circumstance. I wasn't going to change myself to fit in, trading my pretty suits for something less feminine or learning how to speak locker-room. I didn't want to have to become one of them to succeed. Yet the patriarchy was real, and I'd been lucky to dodge it for as long as I had.

What choice did I have?

Weathering the Change

Late that night, I headed home in the stifling humidity. The air felt charged, as though a storm were coming. As I walked, a plan began to take shape. I'd mulled over what it might take to start a translation business ever since my time at Euramerica. I saw what they got wrong, and I knew I could do it better. I always had a Euramerica-style startup in the back of my mind, but figured I'd work in finance for a while, do all my learning on someone else's dime. Then, once I had a nest egg, I'd start my own shop, but that would be years in the future.

But what if I did it now instead? What if I created the opportunity I wanted? What if instead of changing myself, I changed my circumstances?

Hell, I was used to living like a student; what was a little more time not having money? Sure, I wanted to move somewhere better, but after every terrible day in the office, the sad dorm room felt like an oasis. My brain churned with possibilities as I passed the familiar landmarks on my long trudge home.

My MBA program educated me on more than just facts and figures; it taught me how to think and how to break down a complex solution into manageable bits. Looking back, I must always have known I'd start a translation company, because in my rare off-time, I'd been chatting with my old Euramerica friends and clients. I grilled them on the industry, asking them what they thought about the potential for growth. Every single person had a reason to greenlight the idea. I'd already been piecing together those manageable bits, and I didn't even realize it.

In 1992, I saw the trend toward globalization. The growing access to connectivity was changing the face of business. Multinational corporations were expanding. Transportation and communications costs were decreasing. Banking systems were modernizing. Technology was moving forward at light speed. Supply-chain management was improving, thanks to all these factors. The market was right, and relatively untapped. Global business meant the need for global translation services.

I knew two things in that moment:

- We were on the precipice of massive change.
- I could be an agent of that change.

Just the Facts

Today there are 13 million women-owned businesses in the United States, accounting for 42 percent of all companies, per a study by American Express. These businesses generate approximately $1.8 trillion per year.[3]

That night, I called my father to run the idea of opening my own shop past him. I wasn't looking for his financial support—after all, I was incredibly fortunate that he had already paid for college and grad school, and I was so grateful. What I wanted was his opinion. Growing up, he and I had been close, and we shared many passions. We had a history of long talks where he helped me figure out how to navigate the world. He was always a sounding board, and like any great mentor, he coached me to find the answers I needed inside of myself, instead of just giving them to me.

One thing that bonded us is a love of inspiring quotes. In fact, when I graduated from high school, he'd had a calligrapher create an artistic interpretation of many of our favorites. This gesture meant so much to me—a visual reminder of our connection—and it still sits at the center of my desk today. My father often quoted Rudyard Kipling's "If" in times of trouble, change, or confusion, so lines from this poem figured heavily into the calligraphy and his philosophy.

"So, you want to risk it all on one turn of pitch and toss?" he asked.

"I can do this," I told him. "I know I can. Still, I hate the thought of leaving the job and being a quitter. Like you always say, 'Winners never quit and quitters never win.'"

After I floated the idea of starting my own translation company past him, his reply emboldened me. He simply said, "Sounds like you'll probably have more fun if you do that."

Although I didn't need my dad's permission, especially regarding extricating myself from a patriarchal situation, I was touched by his confidence in my abilities. Until Paresco, I'd never run up against an obstacle I couldn't scale, tunnel under, or leap over, given enough hard work. I've never claimed to be the smartest person in the room. **Instead, my superpower has been my will, my grit, my determination.** The secret that no one ever shares is that everyone has the potential to do great things. You can teach yourself to force your heart and nerve and sinew to soldier on, long after they're gone, just as I did. What keeps us down is when we allow doubt to prevent us from trying. Everyone can recover from a failure, but how can anyone expect to bounce back if they never endeavor?

I knew that I had no reason to doubt myself. Before the bank, I'd always found a creative way to bypass an obstacle. Self-doubt hadn't been a consideration, especially over the one factor I couldn't change—my gender. That's when I knew that if I stayed at the bank, I'd lose confidence in my own abilities. I'd no longer trust myself when all men doubted me.

My decision was made.

The next morning dawned clear after an evening of raging storms. The rain had beaten so hard against the soot-covered windows of the dorm room that when I woke up, they were clean for a brief and glorious moment. The whole room was flooded with light.

As I walked up Park Avenue South that day, I had a spring in my step. I found myself smiling at people again, unnerving the other pedestrians as I passed. You see, I'd formulated a plan. Maybe it was risky, but I was ready to fill the unforgiving minute with 60 seconds' worth of distance run.

After exactly four weeks at Paresco, I sat down with James, explaining that I wasn't a good fit for the bank job. He didn't seem surprised, didn't fight for me. If I'd had any doubts about leaving, they'd have dissipated in that moment. I apologized and asked what sort of notice he required. He said, "Two weeks is fine." That meant two more weeks of spreadsheets. Two more weeks of faxing. Two more weeks of idiots yelling, "Schwing!" and "Liz! Phone!!" And I worked those two weeks like I had something to prove; I wanted them to miss my attitude and abilities when I finally walked out of that office and into my future.

On my last day, no one conducted an exit interview. No one cared about my reasons for leaving. No one wanted to take an introspective look at the culture I was fleeing. I doubt they even noticed my final two weeks of frenzied activity. I suspected they chalked me up to a failed experiment and never thought about me again.

Well, that was their loss, because I was off to create a new kind of translation company. A more perfect one. One that was *TransPerfect*.

On the phone the night I'd made my big decision, after my father had said I'd have more fun if I created my own company, he quickly added a caveat: "Although you probably won't make much money," because he was a concerned and protective father and he wanted to make sure I could take care of myself.

However, if you tell me I can't do something, I'll want to do it that much more. This motivated me to work even harder. Fortunately, unlike what was almost always the case, this time he was only half right.

Words of Wisdom

"Living with fear stops us [from] taking risks, and if you don't go out on the branch, you're never going to get the best fruit."

—Sarah Parish

2

Perfecting

An old proverb about success and determination says that the journey of one thousand miles begins with the first step.

The strategy to go step by step became my marching orders for creating TransPerfect, a translation and language solutions company. There were so many moving pieces in the beginning that if I tried to do them all at once (i.e. run until I drop), I'd have been destined to fail. If I were to perfect the process, I'd need to proceed one step at a time.

The First Step

I'd begun assembling pieces as soon as I gave Paresco my notice. My body might have been in the office at 24th and Park during those two weeks, churning out my work, but my heart and mind were fixated on the language services world.

The after-hours chats I'd had with my translator friends became more prescriptive as the clock at Paresco wound down. I couldn't stop thinking about what my philosophy for running a language solutions company might entail. I reached out to everyone I knew, getting opinions on the market and finding out what services their clients wanted. When we'd talk prior to my quitting, I'd ask them theoretical questions like, "In a perfect world, what would your clients want to see done differently?" But once I made the decision to leave, I sought out specifics, like, "What practices could be implemented to help you achieve maximum client satisfaction? Same-day service? A higher commitment to quality?"

If we were to create the world's premier language services provider, the initial steps would entail giving real parameters to the notion of perfection. **My job became taking those abstract musings and turning them into a plan.** If you, say, invent a cure for cancer, it won't change the world if you don't figure out how to take the idea from academic to action.

Words of Wisdom

"Productivity is never an accident. It is always the result of a commitment to excellence, intelligent planning, and focused effort."

—Paul J. Meyer

The Passion Conundrum

I probably should have been overwhelmed at the onset of starting the business. However, I couldn't wait to tackle all the tasks ahead of me because I was fulfilling a promise to myself that I'd never consciously made. I won't say that my working with languages was fated, because I believe we're responsible for shaping our destinies. (In fact, I wrote my college admission essay on the famous quote that man is the master of his own destiny.) Yet I will say things quickly felt like they were falling into place because I was pursuing my passion. The amount of sweat equity needed was staggering. The trick was, because I was excited about and engaged in the subject matter, it didn't feel like work.

My love for languages began when I was in third grade, the year my family moved to Portugal. Until that time, we lived a standard suburban existence in Westchester, New York. Our days followed a neat, predictable pattern, from what day we'd have meatloaf to what time we'd sit down to watch *The Brady Bunch* as a family.

I was small for my age, and shy, but I had a nice group of friends and I enjoyed school. Still, there was nothing exciting or different about my family's life there, save for when we'd travel somewhere interesting for vacation, and we all came to life. A few years prior, there was talk about moving the family to Jamaica so my dad and his friend could open a car rental business. But after a revolution broke out, the plans were scrapped. That's why, when my dad decided to pursue the opportunity to take KFC's eleven herbs and spices across the pond, the whole family was on board.

Upon arrival in Portugal, I felt as though I'd been given a chance to stand out. Instead of being a just another suburban kid, I was instead an *American* and thereby worthy of interest in a place where few Americans traveled. Residents wanted to communicate with me, and I thrived in an environment where I felt unique and alive.

Just the Facts

In 2018, researchers at MIT, Rice University, University of North Carolina, and Columbia University found that living abroad boosts your decision-making clarity.[1] In layman's terms, becoming bilingual actually changes and improves both the gray and white matter in the human brain; it's like going to the gym for your intellect.[2] That's why even if you can't travel abroad, it's imperative to find ways to experience new cultures and new ways of thinking and living.

I picked up the language quickly. Learning languages tends to be easier for children than for adults. The theory behind this is that when you're a child, the rapid neural formation in the brain makes children better at associating new words with meanings.[3] There's also the thought that children aren't afraid of making fools of themselves while trying to speak a new language. Plus, they haven't yet learned complicated sentence structure. That's why it's easier for them to simply pair a word with a meaning, without having to parse out grammatical rules, and the language is more likely to stick with them. The bonus is that early learning leads to having a better accent.

We'd moved to Lagos in the south of Portugal, part of the Algarve region, a beautiful, sun-soaked, windswept area with cliffs overlooking the Atlantic. What I loved most is that I was an entire ocean away from familiar Westchester. No one in Lagos spoke any English, and my parents understood little Portuguese, so I wanted to help bridge the language gaps. I loved feeling as though I brought valuable skills to our family unit.

For me, speaking Portuguese was almost like acting—it allowed me to be another person. I got to try out a new, less shy persona, and this gave me a confidence boost, especially helpful because I went to two different schools there. I got to be the new kid twice, and not just regular old Liz who everyone had known since kindergarten. Because I was young, I was absorbing the language like a small, bell-bottom-clad sponge, so my mother would assign me extra responsibilities. For example, she'd send me to the local bakery to purchase bread for the family. (A word about the Portuguese bread I'd buy: it was golden and crusty on the outside, but light and sweet on the inside. Eating it fresh from the baker's oven felt like a hug on a plate.)

I'd show up at the bakery, wearing my favorite Snoopy T-shirt that read *I'm So Cute*, speaking Portuguese well enough to merit not only the baker's praise, but often an extra treat made just for me. So it's no surprise that I got hooked on languages at an early age. I threw myself into learning more Portuguese, listening to cassette tapes so that I could assist my parents. Soon I was reading signs and truly helping them navigate our strange and exciting new life. I felt a sense of purpose and this was a high I wanted to chase.

After only a year, my father's business brought us back to the United States. And the year after, when I was starting fifth grade, we moved to Toronto, Canada. Two years later, in seventh grade, I was enrolled in a French immersion school. Everything there was taught in French and I loved being able to master something new. In high school, I'd go on to learn Spanish and Latin, which I adored.

I distinctly remember my sophomore year of college when the deadline came to declare my major. I was super stressed out about it. I called my father that night and explained that I loved my language courses the most but felt that I needed to major in something "more practical." He advised me to pursue my passion, major in what I loved, and that the rest would take care of itself. Boy was he right. I'm incredibly grateful for his fantastic advice!

I'd eventually spend my junior year abroad in Spain. That's why the notion of starting a company that focused on my passion for languages made sense both personally and professionally.

However, I must caution you that having passion is but the *first* step to creating your own business, not the *only* step. Recently, Josh Kolbach, CEO and founder of the Rymera Web Co., wrote a *Forbes* article about why following your passion is not enough to be successful. He says that while you may be passionate about something, you may not possess the skills to make this passion a full-time career.[4]

Another problem is that in the quest to follow this passion, you may limit yourself from exploring other opportunities. A brief word about my cultural touchstones—my frame of reference on pop culture is limited, given the hundred-hour weeks I worked for years. Unless it's completely mainstream, I probably don't know it. That's why this makes me think of Adam Sandler's eponymous character in the movie *Happy Gilmore*, where he spent so much time bemoaning the fact that he wasn't playing his beloved hockey—despite his lack of prowess—that he almost cost himself the opportunity to be a professional golfer. (It's all in the hips.)

Kolbach's third point is that your passion might not be goal-oriented, and if it isn't, you need a different plan. I'll address how to hone and harness your passions in a later chapter, but for now, understand that having a passion for what you're doing is a crucial building block.

Words of Wisdom

"Passion is the one great force that unleashes creativity, because if you're passionate about something, you're more willing to take risks."

—Yo-Yo Ma

What's in a Name?

Our very first task was figuring out what to name the company. While all we wanted to do was to start pitching services, we first needed a corporate name to put on the letterhead. In an article for *Business Insider*, Dave Smith discusses the five traits that all great company names have in common.[5]

First, the name must be "sticky," meaning memorable; second, the name should be short. As Smith says, "Brevity leads to memorability." The name also must be functional, meaning it implies the function or service that your company will provide, which definitely eliminated using our own names. What does an Elting or a Shawe even do? Elting-Shawe sounded like Phil and I would be getting into the business of carving sketches of three-masted schooners onto whalebone, likely not a growth industry. Plus, we didn't like the idea of using our names because we thought they would limit us, giving the impression that we were a mom-and-pop shop. The only way my name alone would work would be if I started a knitting company and wanted to call it Elting's Feltings. (There's a reason that even though Wetzel's Pretzels was founded by Rick Wetzel *and* Bill Phelps, no one wants a twisty salted treat from Phelps-Wetzel. Yet admittedly it sounds as though they'd do a bang-up job of practicing personal injury law.)

Smith writes that the name should have a story behind it, and he cites the example of the formerly named Holt Tractor Company. When a photographer noticed that the company's new steam tractor "crawled like a caterpillar" when in use, the founder knew that Caterpillar would become its iconic moniker.

Smith's last parameter is that **the most memorable names invent their own language, which is why you don't do an internet database search—you Google it**. You blow your nose on a Kleenex, cover your scrapes with a Band-Aid, and fasten your kids' sneakers with Velcro. . .even if those aren't the specific brands you buy.

Because our nascent budget included only what was in my rapidly dwindling savings account, we couldn't outsource to branding or marketing people, so we had to brainstorm. Communicating the concept of quality was paramount as errors are simply unredeemable in the language space. We also didn't want to have a silly, cheesy name—we were starting a serious company and we wanted the name to be commensurate with that goal. Plus, companies with the founder's names or initials tend to not be scalable (unless you're making sweaters or delicious snacks). We debated the idea of having a name that began with A so we'd be listed first in the yellow pages, as that was a big consideration back then, but none of the ones we picked sounded right.

We wanted to build a language company that was known for turning around immaculate translations, with the quality of the service reflected in the name. I was and have always been (for better and often for much worse) a perfectionist. Ultimately, we were most inspired by one of the only two word processing programs we used back then—WordPerfect. Striving for *translation perfection*, the name TransPerfect was born.

If, upon naming your fledgling company, your chosen moniker suddenly renders every other potential name nonsensical, you're likely on the right track.

My partner worked with me from the very beginning, yet he was also in the Stern MBA program and employed part-time at a bank. Between his schoolwork, class projects, and employment, much of the initial iterations were entirely on me.

In recounting this story, please note that I will go back and forth between using "we" and using "I," because ours was a partnership and the business would not exist without the both of us and, over time, our amazing employees. While there were countless endeavors my partner and I took on together, there were also plenty of things we each did alone, based on our own philosophies and inspirations. (I would dutifully explain these differences to a judge in a Delaware courtroom 23 years later, but I'm getting well ahead of the story.)

Anyway, once the name question was settled, the company needed a logo for the letterhead, which took a considerable amount of trial and error. I remember how the plastic dorm trash can overflowed with the balled-up papers emblazoned with rejected drafts. I still feel guilty about how much paper I wasted, as this was before recycling was mainstream.

Initially, the logo had interlocking Ts in all black because we owned only a black ink printer. (Like Henry Ford said, you can have any color you want, as long as it's black.) When we did finally invest in a color printer, we made the logo red to grab attention, but quickly determined it looked too much like the Kentucky Fried Chicken branding. Even though I had a pro-chicken agenda, thanks to the life it afforded me in Portugal, we toned it down with burgundy, and we were ready to pitch. . .as soon as we figured out whom to target.

A Windup and a Pitch

To target potential clients, we went to the bookstore and bought print copies of company directories, as the world was still a few years away from the ability to simply Google an org chart. (See? It's a ubiquitous name, even if I were to use Bing or Yahoo! or Duck-Duck-Go.) We put all the names in a spreadsheet and then did the same thing with translator directories—this process went on for years.

So, yes, I quit my well-paying job—with health insurance and a 401K—where I filled out spreadsheets all day so I could fill out spreadsheets for free. The irony isn't lost on me.

Regardless of the drudgery, I was grateful for it because it meant I was pursuing my dream. Every data point I logged felt like empowerment, because I was taking the steps to get everything I wanted. My mom's father was a doctor and growing up she'd accompany him on house calls and do office work for him. She has always been brilliant, much smarter than I am. (She was the valedictorian of her high school class in Altoona, PA, among over 700 students.) She went to Smith College and originally wanted to be a doctor. However, her father said, "You can either be a doctor or a mother." She felt she needed to choose, so she chose motherhood. Fortunately, she ended up having a wonderful career in education. But my point is, I knew how lucky I was that she and my father believed in my being able to do both so I didn't mind the total monotony of inputting data into spreadsheets all day.

At night, to relax after a long day of data entry, I read every sales book and manual I could procure, from *Swimming with the Sharks* to Zig Ziglar's books because I knew the only way to grow TransPerfect was to make my every effort be about sales and impeccable service. Time was of the essence, because it was entirely possible that there was another Liz Elting out there with the same idea as me. (Although maybe she would start that textile company instead.)

Once we collected all the data, we created the package that we would blast out to everyone from all those spreadsheets. We sent a cover letter, along with a list of our languages and our rate sheet. One of the problems at Euramerica was in providing an instant quote for a client. Often, they'd have to wait a day or two to find out what they'd be charged, devastating when time was of the essence. We decided to eliminate that delay right up front by establishing set rates for standard services.

This Is Not My Beautiful Life

While nothing could dampen my enthusiasm, I'd be lying if I didn't mention how grim the early days of TransPerfect were, starting with the perpetual paper jams. I can't imagine a more soul-crushing sound than the plastic *ka-thunk, ka-thunk* of a printer misfire in the middle of a 500-piece mail merge, 12 hours deep into the workday with no end in sight.

There's a scene in the 1999 film *Office Space* where beleaguered employees battle the dreaded error code *PC load letter* for so long that they eventually take the printer out to a field and beat it to death with baseball bats as the Geto Boys' "Damn It Feels Good to Be a Gangsta" plays. I felt the same impotent rage every time the printer malfunctioned. Because it was just the two of us, there was no one but us to fix the machine (or buy us a new one if we bashed it with bats), so we had to become incredibly self-sufficient.

We lived and worked in the dingy little room, where we put in no less than 100-hour workweeks. At least my partner got to leave occasionally to attend classes and go to his part-time job at a bank, where he had access to an entire department dedicated to fixing errant printers.

I'm glad I loved what I was doing, or else the atmosphere would have been too oppressive and demoralizing after the initial excitement died down. That love and passion sustained me; this is why I was able to spend every waking hour working in such a grim environment. Of course, I'd be remiss if I didn't mention that there can be issues when starting a business with a romantic partner (or a family member), but this isn't anything we thought about back then; we had too much work to do.

We had a giant fax machine wedged in the opening of the pass-through kitchen, with a computer and printer on the desk, and the kitchen table was half covered by a typewriter. The room was too small for an adult bed, so there was a twin mattress on a steel frame. For some reason, the only decor we had was a stuffed animal pinned to the wall.

We worked every day from the minute we got up to the moment we went to bed. Did we have weekends? Holidays? No. Just calls and letters and spreadsheets. So often, company founders talk about how exciting it was in the beginning—and it is, because it's so hard to replicate that rush of heady enthusiasm—yet they neglect to mention the sheer volume of hours it took to work for a foothold in the industry. I won't sugarcoat what a grind it was. However, we knew we were working to create something greater than ourselves and we were determined to make it perfect. You control your outcome based on the hours you put in; the more you work, the greater the likelihood of success. The sheer amount of sweat equity is staggering when I look back at it, but that's what it took.

Ask any founder and they'll tell you the same thing.

Words of Wisdom

"The harder you work, the luckier you get."

—Gary Player

Yes, there were times I questioned what I was doing. One early morning, after a restless night sharing a child-sized mattress, I wanted to wake myself up with a bracing cup of coffee. As I went to pour the water into the reservoir at the top of the machine, I opened it up and a swarm of cockroaches erupted from its depths. Like a clown car, they continued to spill out, one after the other in what felt like an endless stream, scurrying out across the chipped Formica countertop at lightning speed.

Oh, was there screaming.

I could have gone one of two ways here. I could either quit and return to the boring but safe, secure, and exterminated world of international finance, or I could take the roaches as a sign that I needed to double down on my efforts and sell enough to get us out of that damn dorm room within six months.

I chose the latter.

I also chose to buy a new coffee maker. There are times that quality of life must come first, and that was one of them.

In the Beginning

The best way to start a business isn't necessarily to reinvent the wheel—**instead, you need only a problem to solve.** The concept of problem-solving is something I studied in B-school, learning how Fred Smith revolutionized the rapid document delivery system by creating FedEx. He didn't invent mail delivery—**instead, he perfected it by addressing the need for urgency.**

In a piece by *Opinion X*, the editors make the point that every tech company you know got its start by figuring out how to solve a specific problem for a specific consumer segment.[6] They use the example of

Facebook, where the original customer was an Ivy league co-ed, and the problem was they couldn't connect with their friends online. On the *Freakonomics* podcast, Mark Zuckerberg said, "You could find music, you could find news, you could find information, but you couldn't find and connect with the people that you cared about, which, as people, is actually the most important thing. So that seemed like a pretty big hole that needed to get filled."[7]

Or take the example of Instacart, the grocery delivery service. The original customer was a working professional in San Francisco who didn't have a car, and who needed a more efficient way to get their groceries.[8] Per CEO Apoorva Mehta in a Startup School NY 2014 presentation, "One thing that has been with me for as long as I remember is the pain of grocery shopping. I have dreaded going to the grocery store. Once you get there, you have to circle through the aisles to find the items that you're looking for, then you have to wait in line to check out and then lug your groceries back to your apartment only to realize that you've forgotten something at the store. This was 2012 and we were buying everything online, but the one that all of us had to do every single week in the most inefficient means possible was [grocery shopping]."[9]

What's interesting in these examples is that the original problem that founders wanted to solve was a small one, for a unique group of people. Yet their ideas were so scalable that they quickly went mainstream.

I wanted to do the same for translation services.

Liz's Life Lesson

If you want to go big, and I think that's the only way to go, then scale up as you perfect.

I looked at all the areas where I determined Euramerica and its competitors had deficiencies, as those would be the places we'd target to differentiate and perfect. One of the biggest failings I saw was exactly what Fred Smith wanted to address—incorporating a sense of urgency. That meant never making a client wait for a simple quote or a longer-than-necessary turnaround time for a project.

I spent a lot of time in the early days calling competitors to do market research. I learned that the competition could take hours or even days to provide a prospect with a quote on a standard service. I saw no benefit in making a client wait, so having a rapid turnaround time became my priority. I needed our potential clients to know that we were there and ready to address their needs, so our policy was to either provide quotes instantly on the phone, or in writing within fifteen minutes for custom projects. While everything required a quote, in the early days we provided a rate sheet that explained how we priced. This set the stage to demonstrate that we'd be far quicker on turning around the project.

Another problem at Euramerica was a disconnect between sales and production. I knew we needed to get everyone on the same team (which is remarkably easy when *you are your whole team*). I didn't like that Euramerica would turn down business when it fell outside the scope of their services. When many of your clients ask for X, doesn't it make sense to create a solution that addresses that need? Why not be a one-stop shop? We didn't want a portion of everyone's business; we wanted all of it. Yet we were also careful enough to know that we didn't want to be too dependent on a handful of clients. We'd mitigate the risk by casting a wide net.

Through my research, supplemented by my experience, I discovered that Euramerica and their contemporaries could be complacent in tending to the business that they cultivated nationally, when there was an entire world outside of North America, desperate for service, a market we'd eventually tap. Once we hung out our shingle, I didn't have to "steal" business from Euramerica, even though I would have been allowed to, because I never signed a noncompete agreement.

Instead, we discovered that there was so much unmet demand in the marketplace that there was no reason to generate badwill by poaching former clients. **It wasn't until we began to fulfill needs that we discovered exactly how deep the needs were.**

You Never Forget Your First Time

I'd just hung up from making my millionth cold call of the day when the strangest thing happened—the phone, which was hot to the touch from constant use—began to ring. I cocked my head like a Belgian Malinois hearing its handler say "walkies," meaning that I perceived that something good was afoot, but I was still somewhat skeptical that the thing I wanted more than anything could be on the precipice of happening.

For a moment, I was stunned that the phone could receive incoming calls, but I quickly pulled it together and answered the ring.

The Demovsky Lawyer Service was calling to see if we could accommodate a small job, translating a three-page contract into Slovak. I was torn between laughing and crying while speaking with DLS, but I somehow held it together, not only long enough to get all the job specifics, but also to find out how they'd heard about us. Turns out they'd received one of our mailings, and I'd had them tracked on our extensive spreadsheets.

Instead of screaming, "I can't believe we pulled this off!" I handled the call like it was one of a thousand I'd received that day. I didn't want them to know they were the guinea pig for all our processes. Instead, I acted like I'd been there before. And here's the thing—I sort of had. I'd been there for hundreds of Euramerica clients and what this client was asking for wasn't anything I hadn't managed previously. But this time, I owned it. I had a plan to work out the bugs. I had the benefit of handling the process from start to finish, to ensure a seamless, Trans*Perfect* experience.

It was only a couple of hundred dollars, but we were on our way.

Liz's Life Lesson

Tell your mom, not your client, that it's your first sale.

Now Do It Again

The second job came in shortly after the first, and that was equally exciting. We were actually doing it! We didn't have *a* client; we had *clients*.

Not long after that, we'd targeted a company called Cyprus Minerals because we'd gotten ahold of their information, and we'd faxed, mailed, or called every viable person in the company, all 300 of them.

Thanks to having blanketed them in enough mailings to melt the polar ice caps, they called us initially, asking for a geological report to be translated into Russian.

Here's the thing—it wasn't enough to have a translator who spoke Russian and English. Because the document was a scientific study, we needed someone who also specialized in geology, which was no small order.

Instead of saying no, we figured out what we would need to put in place so we could say yes. We began calling Russian embassies and consulates, where we eventually found a Russian translator who specialized in geology, and Viktor had the exact skill set we'd needed. Together we'd translate, edit, and proofread this one-page document, making it as flawless as possible. Perfection was our only goal. We didn't want to just provide the translation—we wanted to give Cyprus the best, most accurate translation, delivered with the kind of service one can offer when one's client roster could fit on one's living room couch.

We lived up to the promise of our name, providing what was a perfect translation. While this wasn't the very first step in the 1,000-mile journey, it was an important one. Turns out, treating every client like they're your only client is an effective strategy to build brand loyalty. Unbeknownst to us, the one-page document had been a test for a feasibility study for a joint venture in Russia. The company was so impressed by our quality and service, we won their business on a much larger scale. After that, we found a Russian geologist translator named Gregory who was passing through town, and he ended up coming to the dorm room to work with us on the bigger projects. We hovered behind him, fortifying him with mugs of bad coffee from the new coffee maker and cups of ramen noodles while our cat wove between his feet.

So many miles remained in front of us, but we'd learned to make each step count.

We were on our way.

Liz's Life Lesson

The first million is by far the toughest.

3

Risking

Without risk, there is no reward.
You can't win if you don't play.

The most admired businesses in America today were built by those who risked their own futures and financial solvency to translate their dreams into an industry. In this chapter, I'll explore what it means to take a risk, covering those who gambled and won big, as well as those who played it safe to their own detriment. I'll talk about how a culture of risk-taking shaped who I am and the business we'd go on to create, the checks and balances we put in place to ensure its success, and the one thing you must know above all else.

While I can't make the decision to take a risk for you, I will repeat the adage that fortune favors the bold.

Words of Wisdom

"You only do good work when you're taking risks and pushing yourself."

—Sally Hawkins

Changes in Attitudes, Changes in Latitudes

My early life was shaped by my parents taking the risk to move to Portugal in 1974, a time when going the expat route wasn't so common. The world was far less connected in the 1970s and some of my parents' peers questioned our family's decision, peppering my folks with what-if questions and speculations on worst-case scenarios. But my parents weren't impulsive people, and they weighed all the possible outcomes, comparing risks to rewards, long before they placed any of our belongings in a cardboard box. If my father had his druthers, he and my mother would have moved to Spain in 1961, the year after they got married, to begin importing Rioja wine-based sangria to the United States. (To this day, he regrets that he wasn't the first to introduce sangria to American palates.)

While there certainly were potential downsides, they believed that the upsides of living abroad were too great to pass up. Of course, the 1970s were a more cavalier time, before we worried about car seats or helmets or BPAs, and when it was still perfectly acceptable to smoke on an airplane. (Nope, I am not making this up. There were even little ashtrays built into the armrests!) So, it's possible my folks didn't experience *that* much pushback from concerned friends and family.

Moving wasn't the original plan; instead, my folks wanted to build a home on the coast of Portugal to keep as a villa that we rented out when we weren't using it for family vacations. My dad even created an impressive marketing brochure about the home. But once they started thinking about spending more time in Portugal, they became open to the idea of relocating, and my father was approached with a business opportunity there.

My dad worked in advertising and marketing, but his twin passions were entrepreneurship and wanderlust. He had a desire to see, taste, touch, and smell the whole world, and to bring those experiences to others. In his purview, other cultures were to be embraced, understood, and enjoyed by all, possibly over a generous pour of Rioja. When the KFC franchise started to become a reality, my parents looked at the pros and cons of moving. Even though signs pointed to an imminent Communist revolution, they thought we'd be okay, so we packed our bags and moved to our place on the coast of the Algarve called Casa do Girassol, House of the Sunflower.

Despite my father's extensive education at the Kentucky Fried Chicken training center in Louisville, Kentucky, the Communists apparently did not care for American fast food or their purveyors. Ultimately, he was unable to bring buckets of extra crispy and Styrofoam sides of slaw to the Portuguese people. Fortunately, my mother was able to maintain her career, and she spent her time there teaching at international schools.

Partway through our tenure in Portugal, we moved to Estoril (outside of Lisbon) and that's where things got a bit weird. The Portuguese government didn't believe my father was an actual entrepreneur. Instead, they were convinced he was working not for KFC but for the CIA. Because of this, they tapped our phones and opened our mail, and that was frightening. One night, my parents were having dinner with the US ambassador to Portugal, who was my school friend's father. When my mother said something about my dad working at the agency (meaning the *ad* agency), the ambassador's wife gasped and said, "We knew it!" meaning they knew he'd worked for the Central Intelligence Agency.

Violent demonstrations in our area became commonplace as the Communists rose to power, and my family worried that we'd be targeted. Anti-American sentiment had begun to fester. Still, my father wanted to leave his mark on the country, and before we returned to the United States at the end of the school year, my dad had opened three Italian restaurants called Frascati, which he then sold.

Once we returned to the States, I was braver and more independent for having had our adventure. I had newfound confidence, and that paved the way for me to take a few more chances. For example, in high school, after we'd moved to Canada, I took a job at a dry cleaner in a dicey part of town. The job paid well, and I loved working with people and clothes, so I was willing to walk alone at night and take the subway home late because I felt like the rewards were commensurate with the risks.

After college, I moved to Caracas, Venezuela, to do an internship before finding my first long-term job. Through AIESEC (the International Association of Students in Economics and Business), I headed down there not knowing a soul. I was off to work as a financial analyst at Venezolana de Cementos, which was the largest concrete manufacturing company in Venezuela. While I didn't have much passion for financial analysis (or concrete), I was so excited to hear nothing but Spanish as the plane touched down in Caracas.

Like my dad, I couldn't wait to see, smell, taste, and touch everything in Caracas, immersing myself in the culture. On my first day of work, my coworkers were so delighted to have an American working there that a dozen of them took me to what they told me was going to be a very special lunch. I couldn't wait! It turned out it was at. . .a Venezuelan McDonald's! They assumed since I was American, I'd want American food—a fast-food burger, in particular. Fortunately, I found ways to talk them into better dining spots during my tenure there.

Venezuela was so unlike anywhere I'd ever lived; the standards of living were dramatically different. Sure, my apartment cost only

$50 per month, but I was also being paid $150 per month as the country had been in economic chaos since the 1983 devaluation of the *bolivar*. That's where living within my means became even more of a necessity, a trait that was invaluable as we built our company. The idea of being stuck in another country without enough resources was too terrifying to imagine.

I'd outlined the pros and cons of moving to Venezuela prior to accepting the internship, because I think it helps to see all the factors on paper. I live by the 51/49 rule when it comes to decision-making, meaning that if the pros outweigh the cons by at least 51 percent, I go with the pros and don't rethink the decision. If it's a yes, then it's a yes, end of story.

But that doesn't mean you ignore the cons; your best bet is to find ways to address them.

One of the larger cons about Venezuela entailed the overarching need for prudent financial management, so I made sure to have a budget in place before I left. However, what truly gave me pause was that an engineering student had been killed there after he had peed on a resident's lawn following a boozy night during his graduation celebration. Tensions were high, and protests had turned violent over the spring prior to my arrival. Plus, rampant inflation had drawn a line between the haves and have-nots, and shantytowns were on the rise. While my research showed that it wasn't the best time to be in Caracas, I decided the positives on my list outweighed the negatives. I would just have to exercise caution.

Liz's Life Lesson

When in doubt, list it out. Write down the pros and cons so you can see them side by side. Sometimes a visual cue can help your decision-making process.

I spent the fall in Venezuela working diligently and sticking to my budget. Discipline is a lot easier when there's a modicum of fear attached. While Venezuela was beautiful, it could be a scary place.

As my internship neared the end, I'd planned my reward for my four months of responsibility. I took multiple buses across Caracas to the fancy mall that sold the gorgeous Charles Jourdan shoes I'd coveted since my first day on the job. I'd saved for four months to buy two pairs. I'd promised myself that I would protect my investment, that I'd polish them with special oils and buff them with a diaper before housing them back in their fancy box. I'd planned to keep them forever, and I'd wear them to land whatever big job interview I'd have once I returned to the States. They would be my lucky shoes.

And the shoes were lucky—bad lucky.

When I was almost home, a half block from my apartment, and in the middle of the day, I was held up at gunpoint and robbed. Thieves took my money and my ID, including my passport, as well as my two shopping bags and my sense of safety and security. In retrospect, my day trip was a naïve decision.

I can't say that the risk of living in Caracas paid off financially, as I returned with literally nothing. Though I loved the adventure and wouldn't trade my time there, the experience of coming home empty-handed after all that effort was too powerful to ignore. So I found a "real" job with Euramerica, which led to Stern, Paresco, and a trajectory that was forever altered.

Rolling the Dice

There's a great deal of risk involved when you want to start a company and, sometimes, to keep it afloat. There are times when you've blown through every contingency plan and exhausted every alternative and you can find yourself needing to gamble.

In the case of Federal Express, that gamble was literal, as I'd learn at NYU. Founder Fred Smith's idea for urgent package delivery was a solid one, regardless of what his Yale professors thought. (Smith received a C on the term paper he wrote detailing this idea. Imagine teaching business and being that shortsighted!) Yet Smith wasn't dissuaded from that dream. After serving in Vietnam, he came back to the States to start his company because he was compelled to found a company that could deliver letters and packages that absolutely, positively had to be there overnight. His motto would be that People + Service = Profit.

Fortunately, savvy investors weren't quite as finicky as his professor, and he was able to bring in millions of dollars between loans and equity investments to fund his idea and his company. Per a 2008 article in *Entrepreneur* magazine, Smith had raised an impressive $80 million by 1973.[1] However, FedEx was gravely impacted by the energy crisis, and rising fuel costs plunged the company into millions of dollars' worth of debt within the first few years. They were on the verge of insolvency; by 1974, they were losing more than $10 million per year.

The company had $5,000 left of liquidity in 1974, but Smith had a plan. He was counting on the Board of General Dynamics to give his company the additional funding they needed to keep the lights on, so he went out to meet with them.

But they said no. That must have felt like a kick in the heart.

On his flight back home, Smith decided to risk it all on one turn of pitch and toss, so he stopped in Las Vegas and hit the blackjack tables. Apparently, he was better at cards than he was at writing persuasive term papers, and he won $27,000. He wired that money to FedEx to cover expenses, and although it didn't get them out of debt, Smith took it as an omen that things would get better. They did.

The story of this heroic gamble has grown and changed over the years in the media, but what is absolutely true is that Smith took the chance to bet on himself. Of the experience, Smith said, "No business school graduate would recommend gambling as a financial strategy, but sometimes it pays to be a little crazy early in your career."[1]

While I knew that starting my own company was my own version of a crazy gamble, I had every reason to believe the risk would be worth the reward. Years later, I'd learn that so many of the largest unicorn bets had similar stories to mine. For example, Steve Jobs and Steve Wozniak had no business experience and very little money, but they quit their jobs and started Apple. Jeff Bezos was senior VP at a Wall Street firm—a stable job and a comfortable lifestyle—but he decided to quit his job and start Amazon.com. It all starts with that decision.

When I listed all the pros and cons, I believed that if I set goals, I could work past the negatives. My due diligence told me that if we could innovate, implement the highest quality, and offer a more extensive range of solutions with top-of-the-line service and offices in every gateway city around the world, our business was viable.

However, I didn't have Smith's $80 million in funding in the beginning—and I wouldn't have wanted it if it were offered.

Words of Wisdom

"You absolutely, positively have to innovate, if only to survive."

—Fred Smith

Sometimes You Have to Not Spend Money to Make Money

The one risk I would not take was accumulating debt in the early days of the company in 1992, outside of my credit card balance, and even that gave me pause. The idea of accepting someone else's capital infusion wasn't appealing to me, largely because I didn't want to owe anyone, and I especially didn't want to sell equity. As an entrepreneur, you must consider this decision carefully. My friend Danny Briere, director of the entrepreneurship program at Trinity College (my alma mater), says:

> I have always drawn certain lines that I simply would not cross—it was just too far to go. You can get carried away in a startup. One is that I would never put my house up as collateral on a startup risk. I know so many people who literally lost their houses, spouses, and lives over a startup. Startups are worth the risk, but not worth your life. You need to draw lines to keep it all in perspective. This is one reason why I mitigate risk by having great boards of directors and advisory boards—they help me keep it all in perspective.

Granted, the only assets we had in the beginning were a share of a printer and part of an alley cat, but I knew that fulfilling the growing demand would ultimately be profitable. I was in it for the long haul, aiming to make it the world's leader because it was my passion. But I had to watch every single expenditure, especially in the early days.

Our initial business model involved maintaining a massive database of linguists who could translate and interpret to and from every language in every different and technical field and, after multiple rounds of quality control, reselling their work, making our profit on the markup. In the early days, building this list took more manpower than expenditure.

These linguists are enormously talented. They have the highest level of fluency in multiple languages and a superior level of knowledge of the terminology in their respective fields. On top of that, the translators are terrific writers, the consecutive interpreters have amazing memories, and the simultaneous interpreters have the remarkable ability to listen in one language and speak in another simultaneously. I can't do that in English.

Building this database began with piggybacking off of the ATA (American Translators Association) Directory. However, we saw value in making our database the most robust, so we supplemented this information with names we collected in a variety of ways, from calling consulates and embassies to getting referrals to placing ads. (Years in the future, we'd create a recruiting department to find linguists, and we'd create language certification tests, which led to translators actually coming to us, but I'm getting ahead of myself.) Ultimately, these translators wanted to be found. They were the talent, and they preferred doing the translating itself, rather than marketing their translation businesses. We were able to cover all the languages from the beginning because our translators were subcontractors, hired on a per-project basis, along with editors and proofreaders for rigorous quality control. Even before we scaled, we could take any job as we'd build in the costs for the subcontractors.

Ours was a spartan existence for years in the beginning. Seriously, I'm talking years of going nowhere, waiting for the phone to ring, and nonstop work weeks, fueled by nothing but passion for what could be. We lived on the four-for-a-dollar packages of ramen and cups o' noodles. If we were to really splurge, we'd have the $3.99 dinner at Dallas BBQ and call it a business meeting.

My partner and I figured out that we could backload the cost of the dorm room, not having to pay for it until the end of the semester, so we did that for the entire school year. By the time he graduated, we had just enough money to cover the dorm fees and move to a studio apartment, but not nearly enough money to hire professional movers. One of our buddies was helping us with all the packing. I noticed the friend was tossing stray pennies into the trash instead of boxing them up, and I just went crazy—we needed every cent we had.

For years, we took virtually no salary, just enough to cover our paltry living expenses. At the same time, our B-school friends were living their best lives, working at blue-chip, too-big-to-fail companies like Bear Stearns and Lehman Brothers (ahem). They were going on tropical vacations, getting married, taking summer shares in the Hamptons. The only activity we had outside of work was watching *Melrose Place*. Because we couldn't stop to watch it live, our friend in Florida would tape the show and send us the videocassettes in the mail. I aspired to be Heather Locklear's character, Amanda Woodward (but nicer), as did many of us who were getting started back then. Representation always matters.

I recall in 1996, a full four years after we started the company, we were being interviewed on CNN about starting a company with only your own bootstraps. The interview was the result of someone I'd met through networking. A quick word about networking? In the words of auctioneer and author Lydia Fenet, "Network or die." I met a reporter for the *New York Daily News* at a client dinner, and he was the first person ever to interview us. When I was featured on the cover of *Smart CEO* magazine, that was from networking. A great deal of the coverage we received over the years came through networking. During our CNN piece, it came out that we were paying ourselves the princely sum of $8,000 per year. After four years in business. To live in New York City. (I know, right?) But that's what it took to keep the company under our own control, because to do otherwise would open us up to too much risk, not just because of the debt, but because we didn't want to run out of cash, which is the number-one reason companies go out of business.

Just the Facts
Eighty-two percent of small businesses fail because of cash flow problems.[2]

Cautionary Tales

Because I had such unique experience in the translation space, I didn't want to invite someone else in to make decisions about TransPerfect in exchange for a cash infusion. I didn't want us to become too big to be nimble, to stop innovating, or to find ourselves in unproductive partnerships. You have to understand your own value, especially in the beginning, which is why I knew I'd do what it took to remain in control.

Let's look at Toys "R" Us, for example. In the early days of ecommerce, Amazon offered them a deal where'd they'd be the exclusive provider of toys and baby products for 10 years. Sounds good, right?

Wrong!

Toys "R" Us should have been creating their own ecommerce platform, instead of helping build Amazon's. Per Robert Gearhart on the DCW Group company's blog:

> Amazon used the Toys "R" Us brand, the biggest in the toy retail vertical, to condition American consumers to buy their toys online as opposed to brick-and-mortar stores. At the same time that they were using the Toys "R" Us brand to accomplish this mission, they effectively prohibited Toys "R" Us from advancing their own retail presence, leaving them years behind in development and online innovation. They created and built a market by borrowing the most valuable brand in the space while simultaneously boxing the same brand out of their newly created market. Toys "R" Us was a willing participate [sic] in building the car that ultimately ran them over.[3]

Toys "R" Us ended up suing Amazon—and winning—and getting out of the contract, but the damage of not having their own online entity for years was too great a corporate hit, and the company went bankrupt in 2017.

Of course, as of 2020, Toys "R" Us is back with Amazon, as they now have Amazon fulfill digital purchases. If you're in B-school now, I guarantee you'll study this case.

Weighing risk can be a tricky business. Look at one of the great brands of the last century: Kodak. They were synonymous with film and taking pictures. What people don't realize is that they were the first to develop the filmless camera.[4] Let me say that again—*they were the first*. Instead of taking the risk to try something new, their board decided that introducing the filmless digital camera would impact their bottom line of selling film and developing pictures, so they never did anything with the technology and ultimately went bankrupt in 2012.

Xerox had a similar, albeit less devastating experience. They invented the personal computer, but their CEO thought the future was in making copies, so *they did nothing with the technology*.[5] They eventually made the switch to providing enterprise solutions software, critical in what's becoming a paperless society.

Don't Always Take the Money and Run

As our business grew, other companies wanted to either buy us out or simply invest. But I didn't create the business to sell it—I believed in what we were doing, and I wanted to keep building it. I wanted to accomplish our goal of becoming the world's leader and wouldn't consider selling until we did. Still, I can't argue with those who opt to sell. Look at Robin Chase and Antje Danielson, for example. They're the people who started Zipcar with $68 in the bank. They had the idea for a car-sharing business because they'd seen the same business model work in Germany and Switzerland. Eventually, they sold the business to Avis for $500 million.[6]

Then there's *Real Housewives* alumna Bethenny Frankel who sold her SkinnyGirl line to Beam Global for $120 million, and now she spends her days doing philanthropy with her charity B-Strong. Whenever there's a crisis or disaster, she's among the first on the scene, delivering help and comfort to victims. **There comes a tipping point in ultra-successful people's lives that making another million**

doesn't matter; instead, they want to make a difference in the world. (More on this in Chapter 15.)

Words of Wisdom

"If you're in the luckiest 1 percent of humanity, you owe it to the rest of humanity to think about the other 99 percent."

—Warren Buffett

We believed in TransPerfect's potential, which is why we rejected offers for the company in the early days and over the years. We knew that if we managed our risks, if we stayed lean and set goals, and if we innovated and serviced, we could become a billion-dollar business, given enough time.

One of the reasons we were able to grow without taking on debt has to do with how we paid our salespeople. (I'll get more into specifics on how we hired in Chapter 13.) We brought in a lot of recent college grads and offered a low draw with unlimited upside. The way we paid made our employees feel like they were entrepreneurs, with the unlimited earning potential, yet none of the risks of running their own businesses. They particularly liked that if they came in and excelled, not only could they eventually earn a million per year, but they could also build and manage teams of 50 or more people. When incentives are aligned, the sky's the limit.

As for me, I knew that the more I put into the business in the beginning, the more good I could do later in life. And that's exactly what happened.

Timing can be everything when it comes to taking risks. For example, Facebook made an offer to buy Twitter for $500 million in 2008, but the founders didn't believe it was time to sell. They rejected Mark Zuckerberg's offer, which made it possible for Elon Musk to offer $44 billion for the company in 2022. (Of course, as of this draft, we'll have to see what happens next, as the early days of his leadership have gone. . .poorly.)

In 1998, Google founders offered to sell their business for—say it Dr. Evil-style—$1 million because they wanted to go back to school at Stanford. However, Yahoo! Inc. rejected the offer.[7] Flash forward to 2002 when Google offered the company to Yahoo! again, only this time for $5 billion. Yahoo! had offered $3 billion, but Google countered at $5 billion, and that blew the deal. Today, Google (and its parent company Alphabet) are worth more than $1 trillion dollars, which makes me think that Yahoo! no longer deserves the superfluous exclamation point.

The biggest thing I risked with our company was my time, because it took all of it for many years. While I had plenty of fun, it all occurred under the auspices of the company, whether it was a team-building bowling match, a celebratory dinner after a big win, or a retreat with our employees. I didn't have a life outside of the translation space for the rest of my 20s and into my 30s. The big downside is that I missed out on a giant swath of pop culture during that time, hence my references to Adam Sandler movies. But listen, he just won the Mark Twain Award for American Humor, so he stands the test of time. My point is, I'm terrible at trivia night. No one wants to be on my team.

Despite the hours we were working, it never felt like a chore. I could not have endured this schedule at Paresco. The difference was that we created the kind of corporate culture we wanted, where we became a giant family who worked hard and played hard. By the time our company was established, we'd staffed up a dynamic young team, and any free time we all had, we spent together.

My belief from the very first day was that someday all the work would be worth it. As I made my cold calls by the printer that practically ran 24/7, I would imagine not only what it would take to make us viable, but also how we could build a vibrant and exciting workplace, filled with a team of friends who became like family, and that was a complete joy.

What made the difference and mitigated all the risk was that I was in it 100 percent. Eventually, when it was time to taper back into what was a more "normal" schedule, it was difficult to make the transition, and perpetual motion is still my default mode, but I'm working on it.

Later, I'll get into the one thing that I didn't consider a risk at the time—having a 50/50 partnership and not creating a shareholders' agreement drawn up by an attorney. But I was literally picking coins out of the trash in the early days; how were we going to pay someone's retainer? And even though I'd envisioned and aimed for a billion-dollar business, in the beginning, I didn't want to jinx anything by making a contingency plan for splitting it up when it could have just been us deciding who'd get the stuffed animal pinned to the wall.

If you take only one piece of advice from this book, let it be this— insist on a shareholders' agreement and ideally owning at least 51 percent of the company, assuming there are only two owners. Anyone in a partnership would agree. (Trust me, and more on this in Chapter 14.) Of course, Danny Briere suggests taking this advice one step further, saying, "Approach every contract with the eye that it's going to go badly, and plan for that from the beginning. You will never regret this choice. Most partnerships fail."

Zig Ziglar best sums up the notion of taking risks to advance yourself/your business/your life, saying, "You were born to win, but to be a winner, you must plan to win, prepare to win, and expect to win." I add a caveat to this, which is to get your partnership agreement in writing on day one.

Still, for me, to take a risk is the definition of winning. . .even if you never get to wear those Charles Jourdan shoes.

Words of Wisdom

"There are risks and costs to action. But they are far less than the long-range risks of comfortable inaction."

—John F. Kennedy

4

Growing

If you want to dream big and win, you must be able to grow and to keep growing; maintaining the status quo is never sufficient. Growth allows a company to change and diversify, to remain current, to have the runway to innovate. Growth is key to retaining talented employees and to have the ability to reward them with promotions, perks, and the opportunity for them to expand their own careers.

Growth is *everything*.

Growth is critical to a company's long-term success, so in this chapter, we're going to go in-depth on what we did to build the business from the ground up, and how you can, too.

Words of Wisdom

"Without continual growth and progress, words such as improvement, achievement, and success have no meaning."

—Benjamin Franklin

You Can't Reach a Goal If You Don't Set It

Look around and you'll see talented people everywhere. The world is full of folks who are smart, innovative, creative, and diligent—and many of them know it. Proficient people are often keenly aware of their own ability to shine. However, so many of them fail to make it big, despite their merits, despite their confidence, despite their dreams, despite the fact they're better at what they do than 99 percent of their peers.

What holds these superstars back? What prevents them from meeting their full potential? What's the silver bullet?

Think about your own experiences where the best person didn't go home with the biggest prize. For example, maybe the most pitch-perfect, technically proficient, dynamic singer you've ever heard is still working for tips at some random suburban karaoke bar you went to for your cousin's bachelorette party, yet that popular band you hate is selling out arenas.

Or what about your awkward high school chemistry lab partner—the guy who was always accidentally melting beakers and giving you acid burns—the same person who is now a PhD testifying about science to a senate subcommittee?

Why do some succeed when many do not?

The assumption is that the cream always rises to the top, but this is simply not true. While talent, creativity, innovation, hard work, and a certain amount of luck are key elements, none of these aspects will guarantee results on their own.

So the silver bullet for turning talent and potential into success is. . .goal setting, paired with deadlines and accountability.

Listen, I know goal setting is not a sexy concept, especially when presented with her homely stepsisters, deadlines and accountability, but hear me out. A Harvard Business study found that 10 years after graduation, the 3 percent of their students who bothered to write down their goals ended up earning 10 times as much as the other 97 percent who did not.[1]

Imagine the flex of out-earning your peers 10 to 1 at your next reunion!

Goal setting isn't just having a dream you'd like to achieve and putting it on paper. I've already mentioned you need more than rubber cement, poster board, and back issues of *Vogue* magazine to create your vision. What I used and you need is a systematic plan, and that's goal setting's homerun swing.

Words of Wisdom

"Discipline is the bridge between goals and accomplishment."

—Jim Rohn

Goal setting is where most people get stuck, and there are two reasons for this. First, people often come up with an amorphous goal, such as "I'm going to work really hard because I want to create a world-changing app, or an AI-based technology." The problem is that there's no measurable metric behind goals like this and no timeline. Goals must have a direction and a deadline to be effective. A common acronym in goal setting is to make that goal SMART, meaning Specific, Measurable, Achievable, Realistic, and Timely.

Second, **once you've established that measurable goal, holding yourself accountable to meeting the objective in a timely manner is key.** So many people refuse to be tough on themselves, and that's why they don't see their dreams come to fruition. They allow themselves too much slack. (More on this shortly.) Remember, *time is the enemy*—if you wait too long to get your world-changing app or AI-based tech to the marketplace, a hundred other companies may beat you to the punch. You can't wait around because the benefits of being first are too great.

For me, I didn't want to start just any language translation company. When we decided to create our business, I knew there were literally 10,000 other companies in the translation space. While there were a handful of larger organizations like Euramerica, most of them were one- to five-person shops, started and run by linguists who were so busy translating, they couldn't grow their businesses. We were set on starting a different kind of translation company, to be a pioneer in the space. We wouldn't be satisfied to just *be* in the business; we wanted to create the biggest and the best, the world's leader, with the most versatile and robust solutions and be the most client-centric one-stop shop.

We wanted to disrupt the industry.

Our overall goal was specific—to create the world's premier language solutions company. We knew the only way we'd achieve this was by setting measurable goals with deadlines and holding ourselves accountable for meeting them. When I say holding ourselves accountable, I mean working constantly in the early years, because that is what it took to meet our objectives. We wanted to go big to win big and this is what it took. I wish I could tell you about the shortcuts we employed, but there were none. If you want massive success, you're going to have to put in massive effort, for an extended period of time. And there's nothing sexy about it. It's working to satisfy a goal until you worry you can't go any farther and then pushing on anyway. Going from zero to the largest would entail setting and satisfying thousands of smaller metrics along the way (thousands of steps, if you will).

I've always set goals for myself, even as a kid, long before I understood the concept of goal setting. Because my parents strongly encouraged ambition and valued success, I began working in Toronto when I was 10 years old. Not long after I started escorting little kids to school, I took on a paper route. I was already good at walking, so why not capitalize on that ability?

I noticed that my customers were happier—and my tips were larger—the earlier they received their morning copy of *The Globe and Mail*. While your average 10-year-old wasn't looking to become an entrepreneur, I leaned into the opportunity. I became a tiny efficiency expert, figuring out what could be streamlined in the delivery process. I began to challenge myself to shave five minutes off the time it normally took me to deliver the newspapers. My first delivery route was in a high-rise apartment building. At 6 a.m., I'd run down the steps between floors because I found it saved more time than waiting for the elevator. Then, when I met my timed goal, I'd reward myself with a chocolate chip muffin, funded by the extra money I was making. When I took on an afternoon route, my goal was to finish quickly so I could play Charlie's Angels with my best friend Steffi. (Steffi always wanted to be Jill Munroe or Kelly Garrett, but those who paid attention knew it was really Sabrina Duncan in her sensible turtleneck and leisure suit who got the job done.)

The lure of goal setting stuck with me, and in college I really began to appreciate the benefit. I honed my discipline and aligned my goals. My friends would tease me when I'd get to parties late, but I didn't allow myself to go out until I had completed a certain amount of work. Discipline is not fun, but having discipline made the fun possible. I wouldn't have had a good time if I were there earlier because my mind would be on a term paper I needed to finish. The benefit was that in setting and meeting timed goals, I could be in the moment and have a great time. I could do keg stand without ever feeling guilty that I'd left something undone or having to scramble to compensate. (Full disclosure: I never did a keg stand, but I *could have* and that was what was important.)

I spent my junior year of college living in Córdoba, Spain, a time I consider the best year of my life, until I got married and had kids, of course. Still, Spain was glorious. I loved every second of the experience, truly being immersed in someplace entirely foreign to me. After I'd been there for a bit, I even began to think and dream in Spanish. What moved me the most was that despite hailing from a different culture, our sameness as human beings became so clear. **When you're able to communicate, when you can speak the same language, you bridge worlds.**

Just the Facts

Per the Census Bureau, only 20 percent of Americans speak more than just English, while 56 percent of Europeans are fluent in at least two languages. The estimate is that almost half of the world's population is bilingual.[2]

As I wanted to get the most out of the experience, I worked two jobs beforehand to make sure I could afford it. (Full disclosure: I worked two jobs every summer before each school year.) Sure, it might have been nice to slow down after a grueling academic year and enjoy the brief but sweet Toronto summer, but I knew I had to have a certain amount of money saved to be able to relax and enjoy my time abroad. So I created a budget and set a financial goal. I kept that goal at the top of my mind every time I felt like slacking or buying something frivolous. Because I worked so much, I didn't have much opportunity to spend, anyway.

When I got to Spain, I was able to fully enjoy the experience. *¿Sevillanas? ¿Tapas? ¿Sangria? Si, gracias.* Plus, I had enough savings to take advantage of opportunities for weekend excursions outside of class, such as trips from Córdoba to Barcelona, and a spring break spent traveling by train to Paris, Geneva, Venice, Florence, and Sicily. Discipline will get you a Eurail pass, baby! The best part was I was able to focus on the experience (read: tapas, sangria, and flirting with cute Spaniards), because I wasn't distracted by not having had enough money to support myself.

As they'd cry on the Spanish *fútbol* pitches, "GOOOOOOOL!!!" (setting).

After my post-college internship in Caracas, Venezuela, I returned to the United States with the intention of moving to Washington, DC. I planned to room with a friend attending law school. But first, I'd spend a couple of days with my sister Lynn in New York City, as that's where my flight landed. Lynn worked for Ogilvy, the ad agency. She mentioned that I might be interested in checking out a recent Ogilvy acquisition, a company called Euramerica Language Management. It had been started by a recent Russian immigrant who'd hoped to drive a cab in New York but had unfortunately failed his driver's test. Because he needed something else to do, he started translating, and his business took off faster than you can say *perestroika*.

Words of Wisdom

"I love entrepreneurship because that's what makes this country grow, and if I can help companies grow, I am creating jobs; I am setting foundations for future generations. It sends the message that the American Dream is alive and well."

—Mark Cuban

I didn't yet have a job in DC, so I figured checking out Euramerica wouldn't hurt. (More on the notion of how flexibility empowers success shortly.) This was 1987, so I couldn't just Google them. Instead, I called the company to request information, studied up, and thus was able to nail my interview. When you make the effort, you take control.

My goal was to be hired in sales because I loved the idea of working with clients and solving their problems. Plus, I'd have more financial success if I were to land a revenue-producing position. However, my previous jobs working as cashier in a German restaurant and serving as a computer lab security guard were not considered sufficient experience to join the sales team. Also, there were no open jobs in sales.

Instead, I was hired to work in translation production, managing the process between the clients and the translators, but that didn't stop me from pursuing my goal of making it onto the sales team. My production job entailed plenty of metrics, so I calculated that if I could exceed those metrics, I would eventually be able to plead my case for the sales team. I was confident I could sell services that I loved, especially with the data to back me up.

By the time I transitioned into a sales role, I'd gained so much valuable experience in production that it was easy to satisfy—and then exceed—my quota. Unfortunately, the company was top-heavy in management, so I was able to advance only so far. That's when I decided to pursue an MBA, believing that would be the key to opening more doors, like the one to Paresco. . .which I quickly closed.

So there we were in that NYU dorm room, working at a tiny table, with no money in the bank and a two-figure bank balance, having maxed out my credit cards to buy a printer and a fax machine.

I'd learned the importance of cold calling at Euramerica, and before that, in a summer telemarketing job where I sold subscriptions to *Time* magazine. (Had I worked for *Sports Illustrated*, my buyers would have received the coveted sneaker phone with the subscription!)

We always hear the adage that "sales is a numbers game," and they say that because it's true. I used to track my metrics at Euramerica. (If you're not already doing this with your own sales, please start now!) I found that I needed to make X number of calls or send Y number of letters to bring in Z amount of business.

I worked backwards to determine how many calls I'd have to make and the number of letters I had to send to generate the desired amount of revenue each month. While I was able to use a mail-merge for the letters, I still had to put all the information in a spreadsheet, and once the letters were complete, I hand-signed every one of them. I refused to ever rubber stamp them with a signature because I wanted them to show that we'd provide a personal touch, and this is something I do to this day.

Anyway, for simplicity's sake, let's say that 1,000 calls/letters would typically produce $1,000 in revenue, so that would be my goal. If I wanted to bring in twice that amount, I would have to make twice the number of connections. It's math, not magic. This part of the job wasn't glamorous (or much fun) but I knew it would satisfy the metric and help me create a roster of clients. Once I had the clients, I could then spoil them with service and grow that business by taking it global and the fun would begin. I knew that if I met my numbers, I could determine my fate, and you can, too.

Liz's Life Lesson

Work today like no one else will so you can live tomorrow like no one else can.

It took two months and many thousands of calls and letters, but thanks to setting and reaching goals, we finally landed that first client with the Slovak translation job! Not long after, we brought in a few more small jobs. The second of the clients turned out to be the holding company for Bob Guccione. Such was our level of exhaustion, we were slap-happy, speculating on how we might have to translate *Dear Penthouse Forum* letters for international audiences. We were oddly disappointed to find out it was just a basic business letter.

After we brought in that first handful of jobs, it became clear that the company needed a new goal—to produce enough revenue to get the hell out of that dorm room and into a shared office space, within six months.

We had only a couple of clients in the beginning, but for some reason, they all wanted to stop by our office. Argh! I managed to intercept the first client, meeting her in the lobby of the building. But then a different client came to what he thought was our business address, wending his way through the haze of weed and Grateful Dead posters to deliver a couple of floppy discs. When I realized who was at the door, I quickly hustled him down to the lobby, calling out to my "assistant" Molly to hold down the fort as I shut the door. (Molly was our cat.) Getting an office became my top priority, so we did the math and set the goal.

Words of Wisdom

"What you get by achieving your goals is not as important as what you become by achieving your goals."

—Henry David Thoreau

Once we'd hit a goal, such as moving to a shared office space or a better studio apartment, we'd create a new benchmark, like producing enough revenue to hire an assistant. Every perk earned was based on satisfying a goal. It's significant to note that our company never experienced a massive, miraculous event like something you'd see in a delightfully cheesy Hallmark movie—say, finding the one client who'd change everything, taking us from zero to a billion in the blink of an eye, in addition to saving our quaint family farm. Oprah never discovered us and put us on the map with a single, casual mention. (And if somehow she had, we likely wouldn't have been able to scale up quickly enough to satisfy demand.) Instead, our growth happened in small but steady increments, each leap ahead tied to having satisfied a lesser goal. However, we did land key clients who helped us grow exponentially, but we made sure that no one client comprised too large a percentage of our business.

Because I planned my day by the metrics, forcing myself to make the calls and send the letters, lather, rinse, repeat 10 million times, we eventually won the business of Skadden Arps, a large international law firm. We were establishing ourselves, and the reason we got the job is that we'd been so persistent in calling and mass mailing.

Here's the thing about mass mailings—they can be an effective tool, but only if they're sent repeatedly. Today, you'll want to use focused digital marketing strategies, including email and social media, and this is an area where you must be careful, because you don't want to end up on a spam list and face fines. The point is that repetitive exposure keeps your business at the top of mind. For example, let's say you've recycled 10 different mailers about having your driveway seal coated. You may even curse those pesky seal coaters for having sent you so many brochures because you're annoyed and you want them to stop. But there will come a time when you need a fresh seal coating because maybe you're selling your home and you want it to photograph well, or maybe you got fresh paint on your shutters and now your driveway looks junky. You're most likely to call the number on whatever brochure is still sitting on your kitchen counter because it's expedient.

This is the exact same approach we used with Skadden Arps. Did we annoy them with our frequent mailings? You bet. Still, we kept sending letters because we knew one day they'd need us. If you have a driveway, you're eventually going to have to get it resealed, and if you're a lawyer, at some point you'll require translation services to serve your international client base. The firm had hundreds of attorneys, and we'd hit up every damn one of them. I'm not ashamed that we'd ended up on their radar solely because of the sheer volume of contacts we'd made. (We'd eventually win them over with service, but we'll get to that in Chapter 12.)

All we needed was one attorney to reach for our version of a seal coating brochure. And that's exactly what happened. Recently, I attended a barbecue where I spoke with an attorney at a top-tier law firm and he actually remembered getting bombarded with our letters, as did so many people I've met over the years. Our diligence is why we won the legal solutions business for all of the Global 200 law firms in the world. #sorrynotsorry

Anyway, thanks to our persistence, we found out a firm was involved in an international lawsuit, resulting in what was at the time the largest banking fine issued in US history. The firm needed a bunch of Japanese translators, and could we help them? Absolutely we could! At one point, we had 50 translators from all over the country staying in the Beekman Tower Hotel so they could be on-site every day. This project helped us go from being a $1 million company to a $5 million organization, all thanks to the unsexy concept of goal setting.

Words of Wisdom

"Some of us have great runways already built for us. If you have one, take off! But if you don't have one, realize it is your responsibility to grab a shovel and build one for yourself and for those who will follow after you."

—Amelia Earhart

Accountability Now, Accountability Forever

Goal setting and accountability are two halves of the same coin—they are inexorably linked, and you can't have one without the other. It's never enough to simply decide on a goal; you must hold yourself accountable to satisfy that goal.

Be relentless.

Don't accept a half-assed result. It's human nature to want to be gentle on ourselves. The world is hard on us, so we should be easier on ourselves, right?

Wrong.

Wait—did that sound harsh? It's just that most default to trying to cut themselves a break, but **you're never going to advance if you allow yourself to slide. Meet your metrics. The ability to drive yourself past your comfort zone is the difference between a person who can run incredibly fast and an Olympic athlete.** Fast-twitch muscle and genetics account for only so much.

Do you want the win or not?

In my early entrepreneur days, I realized that we had to manage the business by the numbers and results. My rationale was that if we were working for someone else, they'd have set goals and we'd have been obligated to achieve them. So, it made sense for us to do this for ourselves. I knew that if we ever wanted to be a name in the language solutions space, we had to beat our numbers.

This is where personal grit comes into play.

It wasn't easy forcing myself to make the hundreds of cold calls, and sign letters until I was sure my hand would stay fashioned into a claw forever, but it was necessary to do so every day. To get through, I broke down each goal to the smallest achievable piece. Staring down a daily goal of, say, 500 calls, I'd tell myself, "Once I make 25 more calls, I can have a cup of coffee." Maybe 50 calls after that, I'd reward myself with a brisk walk. And 100 calls after that, perhaps a chocolate chip cookie. Hot beverages and fresh air were no great shakes, as they're something almost everyone experiences every day in a first-world society. No one looks at these necessities as rewards, but they were the only compensation we could afford.

Initially, I tried to keep up my social life with friends outside of the company, but I couldn't do it. I quickly learned that I couldn't have it all—at least not at the same time. I was young and I wanted to have fun, with a vibrant, active social schedule, but that desire would have diluted the goal to create that dream organization. I had to choose. Fortunately, given our growth, we eventually filled our social needs within the company.

I'm grateful to have had enough of an inferiority complex that I was determined to prove everyone wrong, because my business school peers saw my quitting the Paresco job as shocking. I can't say I had no other choice for what I'd do with my life, because I had the privilege of both a college degree and an MBA. My education was my safety net, as was my family. Regardless, I felt and acted as though it were TransPerfect or bust, as I was so motivated by my fear of failure.

After a few years, we set the goal of opening one new office each quarter. This is how the company grew to having offices in more than 100 cities—we set the goals and the deadline and we opened a new office in a new city. We'd hire one person to run that office, and once they hit their revenue goals, which was a consistent number across the board, they were allowed to hire a second person, and so on.

I had the pleasure of having sales trainer extraordinaire Jack Daly as a mentor. One of the most important things he taught me and our team was to write down our goals and then share them with people. His philosophy was that it wasn't enough to have self-accountability; he believed in being accountable to those in our personal lives, too.

Liz's Life Lesson

Say it, set it, do it. And then do it again!

I believe that the setting and doing are 95 percent of the equation, because if you don't set the goal, it doesn't get met. The saying it out loud part is only a tiny piece for me personally, but Jack used to tell me, "If it doesn't get shared, it doesn't get done." My philosophy was also based on what Jamie Wengroff, one of my first and favorite employees, used to say. His refrain was, "If it's to be, it's up to me."

In the beginning, I looked at my list of goals as mine and mine alone, but as the company grew and we began to hire salespeople, we were all about sharing those goals with each other.

In the *Observer*, Thomas Oppong writes, "The American Society of Training and Development (ASTD) did a study on accountability and found that you have a 65% chance of completing a goal if you commit to someone. And if you have a specific accountability appointment with a person you've committed, you will increase your chance of success by up to 95%."[3]

What's especially useful is that Jack's advice can apply to all aspects of life, and not just business. That's why I apply this in my life now to keep myself on track. As an example, let's say you're serious about improving your health and you believe the best way to get there is walking five miles a day. By sharing this goal with your friends and family, you not only set up a system of checks and balances, but you're also likely to find yourself in the company of loved ones who want to join you on those walks. Even if they don't accompany you, they're participating in achieving your goal with every fitness tracker and squashy-sole sneaker they recommend.

Everyone wins.

Getting Bendy

We found we had to be flexible on our path to growth. For example, we were so ambitious about opening foreign offices once we were truly rolling because there was so much untapped business out there. To do so, we followed similar metrics to those we employed for domestic offices. However, it often proved difficult to find the right people quickly enough, so sometimes that pushed back our timelines. Instead of giving up, we pivoted because our end game was being the biggest and best in the industry and that wouldn't happen if we didn't have the proper staff in place. We'd rather have no office than one that would ruin our reputation and brand with poor service. That said, we'd double down on our goals elsewhere to offset what we wouldn't earn in that office.

I'm a huge proponent of hiring like-minded people. I always wanted to bring on employees who shared my vision of what the company could be. I would look for the hungriest employees, those who'd truly take ownership of their accounts and responsibilities, and we would grind to bring in new business.

Our methods were incredibly successful—until they weren't.

Even though our people were the most highly motivated and compensated in the industry and our growth was exponential, we found we started to lose people because of their tremendous workload. There's a point of diminishing returns when no financial incentive makes up for the feeling of being burned out. We had to pump the brakes on our speedy growth, finding ways to remain successful, but not at the cost of exhausting our superstars. One of the ways we addressed the issue of employee burnout was by having employees work different shifts to accommodate time zones, and we aligned incentives thusly.

We wanted to win, but we wanted to win *together*.

What's Your North Star?

Growth comes not only from hitting the numbers, but also from constant innovation, and who would be better versed in what we needed than those on the front lines? So innovation was one of our guiding principles. We were good, but we weren't so arrogant that we thought we couldn't be better.

Innovation was one of our most important guiding principles. We created a culture of ownership, where employees were tasked with treating the company like it was their own. We wanted our team to be the company's eyes and ears, always watching for the next big idea. **The moment you stop improving is the moment you stagnate.** We rewarded our staff with financial incentives and titles for coming to us with ideas, whether those stemmed from their clients or their translators or the marketplace. If there were a better way to do it, it was important to us not only to find out what it was, but also to implement it.

We wanted to differentiate the company by providing the top-quality translations in the industry, so it was imperative to come up with our own testing to make sure the people we hired were detail oriented. The first way we vetted people was via their cover letter and résumé. Applicants whose documents were submitted with even one error were not considered. Harsh, but necessary. We also implemented a writing or proofreading test for most positions, even the sales team, because we couldn't have anyone representing the organization sending out cringeworthy pitches that read, "I hope to *here* from you soon."

We had to up our quality control, which we did through training and enrichment, eventually creating an entire department to manage the process, assuring continual improvement. We were dealing with companies that needed more than just a word-for-word translation, so as not to blunder like the classic example of how the slogan "Come alive with Pepsi" translated to "Bring your ancestors back from the dead" in other languages. (I swear I'm not making this up.)

Our reputation was everything and our translators were the talent, so to maximize both, one of our sales leaders recommended that we become ISO certified, because this was recommended to them by one of our clients. Then we completed annual reviews to make sure we still merited the certification. ISO certification is a process certified by a third party, meaning an organization meets the standards developed by the International Organization for Standardization, and it's the key to doing business with regulated industries like life sciences and finance. If, after all the controls we had in place, we still produced an error, we had a checklist to resolve the issue through acknowledgment, apology, and an action plan.

Speaking of innovation, Apple is arguably the world's most innovative company. They actively empower their creatives by giving them all the tools they need to innovate. For example, their industrial design group is housed in an area with restricted access and unmarked doors for extra privacy because management doesn't want anything interrupting their flow of creativity, including the interruption of an unwanted knock on the door. In fact, the entire Apple org chart is arranged to maximize creativity and not restrict ideas. Joel M. Podolny and Morten T. Hansen in the *Harvard Business Review* explain, "Giving [Apple] business unit leaders full control over key functions allows them to do what is best to meet the needs of their individual units' customers and maximize their results, and it enables the executives overseeing them to assess their performance."[4]

Maintaining the finest client service in the industry was another of our key differentiators. Our purpose was to exceed expectations and to delight the client (which I never called the "customer," much like Disney insists on calling visitors "guests") providing the fastest possible turnaround time with the fewest errors. If there were a deliverable the client wanted that we didn't provide, we'd never say, "Sorry, we don't do that." The words *no* and *can't* were not in our vocabulary. Instead, we'd figure out ways we could accommodate them, such as adding 24/7 service and constantly updating our product offerings. If you want to grow, make "yes" the most frequently used word in your vocabulary.

Words of Wisdom

"If you can dream it, you can do it."

—Walt Disney

Another guiding principle was that of frugality. We started with no funding, so we had nothing to fall back on, save for meeting our goals. Scalability proved to be our superpower because we never spent what we didn't have, unlike so many other businesses that started—and failed spectacularly—in the splashy dot-com 1990s. Anything we earned went back into sales and marketing, not foosball tables and Aeron chairs. As the years went on, we lived by what Polonius told his son Laertes, "Neither a borrower nor a lender be." I just don't believe in racking up excessive debt. We ran lean. Fortunately, Molly required us to pay her only in canned tuna. (To reiterate, Molly was a cat.)

I realize I'm beating the drum about working extraordinarily long hours and keeping a tight rein on your cash flow. None of this is inherently enjoyable. Taking the day off and buying yourself something shiny with the spoils are some of life's greatest pleasures. But like those Olympic athletes who spend years waking at 3:30 a.m. to get in an extra morning practice, what they're honing is the ability to grab the gold when the time comes. You're not sacrificing; you're preparing yourself to be a winner.

Do you think Michael Phelps mourns all those times he didn't sleep in when he counts his 28 Olympic medals and $100 million in net worth?[5] My guess is no. Instead, I imagine he basks in the glow of having achieved what no one else has.

So, back to pinching pennies.

The mentality of frugality was freeing and allowed us to concentrate on what was important. Instead of spending time writing up business plans, trying to get outside investment, we focused on bringing in new clients and using that revenue to cover our expenses.

While remaining on our own was initially more difficult than just cashing someone else's check in exchange for a portion of the ownership, it meant that we'd never be accountable to anyone who didn't found the business. That freedom was so important to us. We didn't want outside forces coming in and second-guessing our vision, and we weren't excited at the prospect of selling our equity.

That said, there is plenty of value in considering taking venture capital. Having other people with a vested interest in your business means they will open their networks, expertise, and resources to make you successful. It's usually not the case that VCs try to take control and second-guess your vision. But for us, we knew we were onto something big, and we weren't about to share it with anyone who hadn't contributed the sweat equity.

Let them earn their own brisk walks and cups of coffee.

Words of Wisdom

"Being an entrepreneur isn't really about starting a business. It's a way of looking at the world: seeing opportunity where others see obstacles, taking risks when others see refuge."

—Michael Bloomberg

I Spot a Trend

If you want to grow, you must know what's happening not only in your industry, but in the world at large. That's why trendspotting was another of our guiding principles. One of the smartest things you can do is to keep a keen eye on trends. Look at the example of Borders outsourcing their online sales to Amazon, back when Borders didn't see the trend of online shopping. While they were busy focusing on "the bookstore experience," Jeff Bezos was quietly changing the entire industry. By the time Borders realized their mistake, it was too late. They had to liquidate and file for bankruptcy, closing almost 400 stores and laying off more than 10,000 employees.

In our case, much of the trendspotting came directly from employees and clients, both from feedback and surveys, as well as innovation contests. Our first big deal came from having recognized the trend toward globalization—in fact, this was the biggest reason for creating the company. As the world became more connected, we knew that new markets would soon open. Back when we were just a two-person shop, we pitched JCPenney as they ventured into the Latin American market, expanding into Mexico and Chile. They needed everything translated into Spanish, from labeling to marketing to legal. The purchasing department allowed 30 different translation companies to bid for the business, and we made it to the second round, where we competed against 6 other companies.

In trying to land the business, we flew to Plano, Texas, to meet with the purchasing department. If we were to win their business, I didn't yet know I'd need to liaise with and manage 75 different relationships because everything had been so decentralized back then, with aspects being manned by so many disparate departments.

I felt incredibly nervous walking into this meeting, knowing that they could be our first million-dollar client. But I was certain that if we were to get this business, we'd spoil them with quality and service. That gave me the confidence I desperately needed as I apprehensively entered that boardroom and began my pitch. We aced that round, and then it was down to us and one other organization.

What tipped the scales toward TransPerfect was that commitment to exceeding their expectations, delivering a higher-quality product faster than anyone else, thanks to our rapid turnaround times and 24/7 availability that no one else could promise.

We won the business, and I figured out how to handle all the separate points of contact. We were on our way to the kind of growth that no one else imagined.

Except for us—explosive growth was our plan since day one.

By setting goals, holding ourselves accountable, pivoting when needed, and having guiding principles, there was no way we couldn't win. And if you follow these rules, there's no way you can't, either.

Words of Wisdom

"I hated every minute of training, but I said 'Don't quit. Suffer now and live the rest of your life as a champion.'"

—Muhammad Ali

5

Overcoming

Everyone knows that one obnoxious person from college, that guy or gal who lived down the hall from us in the dorm. Despite being born on third base, this person perpetually thought they'd hit a home run. No one at the 20-year reunion is ever surprised by their success because the way was paved for them long ago.

Unfortunately for the trust fund kids of the world, they're never going to learn that the secret to success is as much about what you've overcome as it is about what you've achieved. Sure, most of us would opt for a smooth sail from our first day on the job to our retirement parties, but it's rare not to face choppy waters. Most people don't have the benefit of having been born into privilege. The true pros are those who find a way to navigate dangerous waters and come back stronger than before.

Words of Wisdom

"Obstacles are those frightful things you see when you take your eyes off your goal."

—Henry Ford

World Piece

Even the biggest and best companies have had to overcome moments of uncertainty or dramatic business shifts. For example, look at the Danish brand LEGO, the iconic maker of those plastic snap-together blocks that are always seeking out unsuspecting parents' bare feet in the night. Everyone knows LEGOs; it's a household name and one of the most profitable manufacturers in the entire toy industry. In fact, my own son's great love of LEGOs almost kept him out of preschool. On the day of his interview (I know, I know, but it's a New York thing), he was so excited to see a tub of LEGOs that he lunged into them headfirst. I was certain my 14-month-old would be shut out of preschool.

What everyone might not know is that in 2004, right around the time my son was perfecting his swan dive into the block tub, the company was on the brink of bankruptcy after they posted a $174 million loss.[1] As a company that had never once posted a loss from its inception in 1932 to 1998, they suddenly found themselves almost $800 million in debt by 2003.[2] Their ventures into theme parks and children's clothing and jewelry had proved to be poor investments, and they were losing ground in the toy market due to the rise in digital play.

What turned the company around was their ability to pivot under the leadership of new CEO Jørgen Vig Knudstorp. He found that the status quo wasn't working, nor were their efforts thus far to diversify. Instead of giving up, he led the company to take different risks, continuing to try to find what *would* work. I closely associate this tactic with how the Lillian Vernon catalog company would operate; their strategy was always to perpetually try new things, keeping what worked and ditching what didn't, retaining something like 85 percent of what they tried. The best way for a company to grow and change is to keep taking those calculated risks.

If you've stopped taking risks, you're abandoning potential growth.

Words of Wisdom

"I never let my mistakes defeat or distract me, but I learn from them and move forward in a positive way."

—Lillian Vernon

Previously, LEGO had partnered with Lucasfilm to produce Star Wars branded sets, eventually creating a Star Wars video game, and this partnership was the only thing keeping the company from going under during the turbulent early 2000s. Making the wiser choice to lean into what was working, they took the success they found in co-branding, moving on to partnerships such as with the Harry Potter universe. Then they shuttered what wasn't gelling and streamlined their production processes in a turnaround bid. Eventually, LEGO came up with all kinds of partnerships, some of which can still be found in boxes or on display in my sons' rooms, such as Yankee Stadium, U of M's Big House, and the White House. The more LEGO diversified with these partnerships, the more they paid off.

While these actions were incredibly helpful, one of the biggest reasons they improved and flourished was finally embracing crowdsourcing from LEGO fans, a practice the company had not previously done. **It's such a simple concept, asking your customers what they want,** but this had never been part of their corporate culture.

Now LEGO keeps up with trends by traveling the world to talk to children and parents, and watching kids interact with the products. This is a practice I believe that every company must undertake. The effort's paid off; by 2012, the LEGO Group surpassed Mattel to become the world's most valuable toy company.[3] They've been recognized by the RepTrack Company as the most reputable brand in the world, and consistently make the top 10 of the world's most recognized brands.

My office is in midtown Manhattan and I pass the LEGO store in Rockefeller Center constantly. It's not unusual to see people waiting in a two-hour line to enter the store, thus ensuring shoeless parents will be yelling about "@#$%ing LEGOs!" for generations to come.

So when your foot comes into contact with a stray block and you have to hobble to the couch, remember, you're stepping on a success story.

Moment of Impact

Facing adversity with grace is a trait common to the most successful leaders. Their ability to overcome is their origin story, a real-life version of what you'd see creating a superhero in a Marvel movie.

My own origin story happened when I was in elementary school. My sister and I were at sleepaway camp during summer vacation back in 1976. I was profoundly homesick. I spent the first four weeks hiding under a blanket with a flashlight at night, writing tear-stained letters to my parents. I didn't want to weave lanyards, I wanted to go home, so I was excited by the prospect of my mother coming up halfway through the summer. I figured I could make my case to leave with her. On visiting day, my sister and I were expecting brownies and instead we got news of my parents' impending divorce. That Bicentennial summer, my parents were declaring their independence from each other.

We were also in the process of relocating, heading from Chappaqua, New York, to Toronto, a year after we'd returned from Portugal. This involved our moving to yet a new country and a new school up in Toronto. I started at the Jesse Ketchum School, where all classes were taught in English. That's why in seventh grade, my parents switched me to the Toronto French School. They also liked the idea of my attending an international baccalaureate school, meaning the curriculum was rigorous and internationally recognized. Eight out of my ten classes were taught in French, and almost all my classmates had started in kindergarten and had at least one native French-speaking parent. To accommodate, for the first two trimesters, I was placed in a total French immersion classroom.

Full disclosure: I had been happy to leave Jesse Ketchum as I'd had a mortifying experience there. In sixth grade, I had a weekly music class, composed of about 60 students in two combined classes. We were performing a song from *Joseph and the Amazing Technicolor Dreamcoat*, which I loved, so I was having the best time singing. The choral director slowly went person by person, to listen to each of us. I assumed she was trying to find a soloist. She stopped in front of me and yelled, "It's you!" I was super excited. But she wasn't looking for a soloist; she was looking for the person who was so off-key.

Instead of having me mouth the words or stand in the back, I was kicked out of chorus and had to go sit by myself in an empty classroom for every single music class for the remainder of the year. Everything is mortifying at that age, so being singled out like this was devastating, but I refused to have someone else dictate who I was. (In this case, a bad singer.) In my ultimate act of protest, I bought the album and sang it at the top of my lungs in my bedroom. Years later, I made sure we'd have karaoke at every company party possible, where I'd perform my go-tos: "Girls Just Wanna Have Fun," "I Will Survive," or "Living on a Prayer." Sometimes being the boss means finally getting what you always wanted.

The summer before I was to begin tenth grade at a new high school, North Toronto Collegiate Institute, I was at our family's vacation home in Vermont. My cousin Heather and I were perusing the shops on the main drag of the sleepy little village of Manchester on a lazy summer day. Heather and I crossed the street and what felt like out of nowhere, I was struck by a car, thrown into the air, and landed on my head. Even now, I can't describe much, as I completely blacked out and have no recollection of what followed.

The impact fractured my skull and broke one of my legs. The other leg ended up being severely injured. The extent of the damage was so bad, I had to be taken by ambulance from the hospital in Bennington to Albany, New York, where I spent the next three days in a coma. There was a boy who was my age in the hospital with the same injury as mine—a fractured skull. He'd been riding his bike in Albany and had been hit in a different accident. For three days, my parents and the boy's parents prayed together, hoping for a miracle.

Only my family received one.

My accident happened on a Tuesday. I finally woke up on a Friday, and when I did, I was speaking French. I spent the next few weeks in the hospital, finally returning to the Vermont home with two damaged legs and hearing loss in my right ear. I was incredibly lucky, not having had a traumatic brain injury, paralysis—or never waking up. I was immobile for the rest of the summer, spending my days exercising my brain by playing Simon, the light-up memory game that was so popular back then.

When we got back to Toronto, doctors discovered that mine was a Salter-Harris fracture, meaning it involved the growth plate, and it had been set wrong in New York. I was so fortunate that Dr. Salter himself was based in Toronto and was my surgeon. He had to rebreak the bone to get it to heal properly. While having him take care of me was best-case scenario, I had to begin the recovery process all over again.

High school is rarely easy for anyone; that's a universal truth. The few who thrive often are adults not worth knowing now. What makes high school a million times harder? Being new in tenth grade, a year younger than anyone because I had skipped eight grade at the Toronto French School, and suddenly disabled. I was stuck in a huge cast for months. To compensate for the cast, I needed a special shoe made. I wanted to look cute, so we went to a Bass shoe outlet and got a pair of suede saddle shoes, which were popular at the time. Technicians had to add a four-inch platform on the bottom of the one shoe I was able to wear, rendering my cute shoe ridiculous. I needed crutches to walk. As hideous as you may imagine this, with my leg cast creaking and my crutches thumping and my bizarre Frankenstein shoe, I promise it was worse.

While already petite, my weight dropped from 90 pounds to 77. I was a living skeleton and I looked haunted, not the cute girl impression I'd hoped to make at my new school. The accident robbed me of my confidence. I became painfully shy, as I was unrecognizable to myself. Keep in mind, the year 1980 was a different time in terms of providing access for all capabilities. The United States hadn't yet ratified the Americans with Disabilities Act, nor had Canada enacted their own version; ergo my school wasn't handicapped accessible. Every day, after being picked up by the special-needs bus, I hobbled into the building and stomped up and down the stairs. My cast was so heavy and thick, I looked like an informant that the mob was halfway through fitting for cement shoes.

Of course, the other kids looked at me with disdain, and they often laughed; how could they not? Being *other* is contagious, and those in the know wanted no part of it. My movements were slow and deliberate, due to the cast and the pain, so I never made it to class on time. My school didn't have an elevator, and I had to manage three stories of stairs between every class. I lived in mortal fear of falling. No one at the school thought to assign me a helper or a buddy, so I carried my own heavy textbooks in a backpack that threw off my balance. My lateness was a fresh humiliation six times a day, five days a week. The worst of it involved biology, chemistry, and physics classes. The science classrooms were arranged in two-person workstations. Being the last one to class every day meant being the only student never paired up with a partner to sit with and for experiments.

In a time when I'd have been happy to fade into the background, I was inadvertently thrust into the spotlight, again and again. I was always alone at my new school. I had no friends. Kids were afraid of me, worried that some of whatever was wrong with me might rub off on them. I was ostracized from the pack, so I spent every lunch hour hiding in the bathroom, eating my lunch in a stall. Let me repeat, tenth grade was a bear. Yet I had no choice but to push through it. The only respite was Mr. McNeil, who taught my Latin class. I liked how he taught and he was always funny. He used to say, "Don't put the em*pha*sis on the wrong syl*lab*le," so his class was the one bright spot in what was a bleak existence for a semester.

While now I know how incredibly lucky I was, at the time I didn't understand why my parents didn't swoop in to save me. Instead, they told me, "Liz, this is temporary. You have to make a plan for your life after this." They encouraged me to stay busy, telling me to keep studying, reading, learning, focusing on my countdown to normalcy. They didn't want me to dwell on my misery, instead encouraging me to be positive, to start planning my life post-healing and my college career. Their message was that I had dodged a bullet, and every day moving forward was a gift that not everyone received. They must have been thinking of those grieving parents in Albany.

During those days stuck at home, I took their advice. I taught myself to cook, going through 25 volumes of a cooking encyclopedia, experimenting with different recipes and techniques. I was living with my mother at the time, and she and I would take turns cooking for each other. We'd have the nicest chats over my chicken croquettes or Wiener schnitzel or her spaghetti Bolognese or cornflake chicken. When I'd see my dad, we'd have lengthy conversations about language and inspirational quotes, instead of focusing on what I'd lost.

Now I see that in teaching me to be self-reliant and grateful, not to dwell on what I had to overcome, they were actually saving me. I've held these important lessons closely ever since then.

Words of Wisdom

"Disasters will always come and go, leaving their victims either completely broken or steeled and better able to face the next crop of challenges that may occur."

—Nelson Mandela

However, what truly saved me, what made me feel capable again, what gave me back my sense of purpose and identity, was work.

Striding into the Future

Freed from my cast, and without the burden of an active social life—having made no real friends the entire first semester—I needed more to fill my evenings and weekends. Also, my parents had stopped paying for anything outside of schooling, food, and shelter, believing my sister and I wouldn't appreciate luxuries if we didn't earn them. All I knew was I wanted to replace my hideous saddle shoe with something pretty. I needed a job once I was healthy enough to stand on my own two feet again.

I was hired at Cadet Cleaners, a dry-cleaning chain. This is where I first fell in love with clothes. Even though it was panic-inducing to sort and tag giant piles of clothing, especially with 20 impatient customers lined up out the door, I always managed to notice the finer pieces. The idiom *clothes make the man* rang true here. The people who seemed the most successful brought in the most beautiful items. I adored handling all the women's clothes, boasting labels from exotic designers like Gucci, Alaia, and Prada. Before I enveloped the cleaned garments in the thin, clear plastic bags, I'd run my hands over impossibly airy silk chiffon blouses with shiny mother-of-pearl buttons, impeccable linen trousers with razor-sharp pleats, the softest cashmere sweaters in a myriad of jewel tones. I recall complimenting one particular customer because she perpetually brought in stunning bespoke garments. I assumed she ran the place where she worked, given the way she dressed. But I learned she didn't, at least not yet. She's the woman who told me her philosophy was to dress for the job she wanted, not the job she had. I nodded, smoothing the rough traffic-cone orange cotton smock I was forced to wear over my street clothes. I promised myself I'd heed her advice someday. Wearing the right thing struck me as a shortcut to acceptance, so I poured my earnings into procuring pieces that might elevate my status, or at least get someone to talk to me. My plan worked, and by the second semester I started making some friends.

After I learned to run the counter, I was sent to work at different stores. One shop was located at the intersection of Jane and Finch in

Toronto. The neighborhood was sketchy. The shop kept a knife taped to the wall behind the cash register that I was told to unstick for use in case of emergency. (Oh, Canada. Never change.)

I guess that's why whenever I hit roadblocks once I started TransPerfect, they seemed surmountable. If I could muscle through tenth grade, I could push through anything, especially years later.

But I'm getting ahead of myself.

The Work-Around

Naturally, there were obstacles to overcome, especially in the beginning when revenue was growing, but not yet enough to bring on the people we needed for key roles, such as IT. We wore every hat, which wasn't easy. Hiring (which we'll delve into in Chapter 13) was a challenge and we struggled to find the right people. For example, when the company first moved to a small, shared office space, we hired a talented bilingual project manager we'll call Tamara. The building required us to empty our own trash cans, something the rest of us did willingly, every day. However, Tamara refused to do this, which was profoundly frustrating. Everyone else was on board with taking out their own trash, but she flat-out refused.

The first key to overcoming an obstacle is to learn from it. My interaction with the diva we'd hired was a real wake-up call. It wasn't that I had to haul an extra Hefty bag to the trash chute myself; heck, I welcomed the opportunity to get up from my desk. Instead, it made me realize that someone who wouldn't even make a minimal effort to do what everyone else would was never going to be a contributor to creating a world-class organization. I learned from making the mistake of hiring solely based on talent, not yet understanding that attitude was at least as important.

When people tell you who they are, listen.

Liz's Life Lesson

Attitude is just as important as aptitude, possibly even more so.

In the mid-1990s, no one wanted to work at a startup like they would a few years later at the beginning of the dot-com boom. Ergo, we had a lot of issues finding talent. Because of our growth, people had to work crazy hours, so even if we did find the right people, we were burning them out with all-nighters. This led to morale and quality issues, which was an even larger problem from which I had to learn. Initially, I thought we could keep them with generous bonuses and high commissions. However, after losing so many fantastic people, I learned the hard way that we needed to implement ways to make sure they had a proper work-life balance.

Keep in mind, a business doesn't have to be a powerhouse for it to have an impact later. Look at the company Traf-O-Data, for example. Wait, you say you've never heard of them? Oh, then perhaps you've heard of its founder, Bill Gates. This was Gates's first business venture. The company went under because Gates couldn't solve the technical problems quickly enough to be useful and having municipalities as a client base proved to be too problematic.[4] However, he saw it as a learning experience and credits its failure with his future success with Microsoft.

My point is that your experience can be as valuable as your bottom line.

Mad Money

The second lesson my accident taught me was to focus on what I *could* do in the moment, instead of what I couldn't do. For example, it was always my goal to become an international organization, with offices all around the globe. The temptation was to build out and blanket the globe with TransPerfect offices, but it wasn't initially feasible financially because we didn't want to take on debt. Running out of cash is the death knell for a new company.

So often, this is where companies fail—they expand too quickly. Look at Wise Acre Frozen Treats, a company started by Joe Picariello. He specialized in making frozen organic popsicles back in 2006 when the quest for organic foods was exploding, producing them in a schoolhouse kitchen.[5] His nascent company was the first to make a frozen treat using unrefined sweeteners. At the time, no other business was using honey or maple syrup, so everyone was suddenly interested in his product, as places like Whole Foods had stopped being simply the place where hippies bought hemp and had come into the mainstream. Hemp for all!

Picariello went from being a one-man show to bringing on 14 new employees in a six-month period and expanding into a 3,000-square-foot processing facility.

Great, right? Wrong!

Picariello ran into trouble because instead of starting slowly and ramping up, he invested money he didn't have on staffing and capital equipment, based on a handshake deal he had with a local billionaire. When the stock market crashed in 2008, the billionaire pulled out of the deal, leaving Picariello holding the bag on equipment he couldn't afford on his own and a staff he couldn't pay, despite having stores that desperately wanted to carry his product.

Per Picariello, "By the end of 2008, Wise Acre had gone out of business. Even though the orders were still coming in, we couldn't pay our bills. The $300,000 bank loan was in my name, and I had to declare bankruptcy. Now the bank owns the product, the equipment and all of the trademarks."[6]

My heart breaks for Picariello, especially because the hardest part is getting the sales and he accomplished that. If I were mentoring a business like his, my first piece of advice would be not to spend what you don't have. I wouldn't allow the entrepreneur to put all their (organic, pasture-raised) eggs in the billionaire's basket, because there should always be a Plan B in place. (And never make assumptions on a handshake—a signed contract is a must.) I'd have advised the CEO to develop a relationship with the bank, lining up loans and lines of credit, and getting multiple investors on board before it was needed.

My advice is always to grow carefully. In this case, instead of hiring so many people and buying space and equipment, I'd have advised him to lease space and equipment in a commercial kitchen until he had the cash flow to expand. I'd also suggest having the clients commit to paying an up-front percentage of the sales—a deposit to cover the operating costs to create the product. Never be so anxious for sales that you place your company in a precarious position to attain them. It often doesn't pay off.

While plenty of companies gambled with and won with a rapid expansion plan, that wasn't in my comfort level for our company. Whether we were opening an office in another American city or overseas, each had to reach a certain benchmark before we'd invest more capital. In the early days, every office was opened by one person, and they'd have to meet a revenue goal to hire a second person, then those two would have to meet another revenue goal to hire a third person, and so on. This is how we grew exponentially, yet still within our means.

Not every risk is worth taking, especially when the wrong one can bring down everything you've worked to build.

Clear Eyes, Full Hearts, Can't Lose

Something that's so important to me personally, and the third lesson of overcoming, is to remain optimistic even when things feel dire. Years ago, Matthew, one of my employees, and I had a pitch at Gateway in South Dakota. This was a big deal for us and would have helped us grow exponentially; all we had to do was nail the pitch.

Because we wanted to be fresh, we left for South Dakota early with the anticipation of arriving with plenty of time to rehearse our presentation and then have a nice dinner and a good night's sleep before our meeting the next morning. The weather? Well, it had other plans. After multiple delays, we were caught in torrential rains with such turbulence that we thought the plane might go down. We even tried to contact our families from the air—this was back when planes had phones on the backs of the seats—so we could say our goodbyes. (It's my theory that everyone believes in a higher power on a bad flight.) Eventually, we were rerouted and then had to take a puddle-jumper, which couldn't get us to our ultimate destination, so we ended up having to rent a car in the middle of the night and drive through cornfields in this hell storm.

The easiest thing would have been to pull into a clean, comfortable Hampton Inn on the side of the highway, shower, cry, and regroup after a good night's rest and miss the meeting. But that's not what happened.

We pressed on.

What kept us going was the belief that if we could make it to the boardroom at Gateway, we'd win their business. We knew that if we dwelled on how bad the trip was, we'd blow the opportunity and our suffering would have been for nothing, so we tried to maintain positive attitudes. We pushed past our sleeplessness and our terror. We arrived at the hotel, fortified with nothing but gas station snacks. We had enough time for a couple of quick showers before we had to go to our 9 a.m. meeting. The key here is that we walked into our meeting with all the optimism in the world. And, yes, we won their business, even though I didn't want to look at corn for a while after that.

Instead of giving up, we used the fear and discomfort to fortify us, saying, "If we can live through this night, we can certainly get through a PowerPoint presentation."

If our experience weren't enough of an argument for using positive thinking to overcome an obstacle, remember that optimists live longer, have better love lives, experience more success, take fewer sick days, and tend to bounce back faster and stronger, using any failure as a fuel for better performance in the future.[7] It can be as easy as reframing something awful, saying, "I can do this," instead of saying, "I can't."

TransPerfect had been growing and prospering, so in early January 2001, we brought all 200 of us together from around the world for our holiday party at the top of the World Trade Center. The night was so magical, we immediately booked that same space again for the following year.

The final lesson toward overcoming is always to have a plan for when things go off track. The need for a plan became crystal clear one sunny day in September 2001.

Our office was located at 34th and Park, two blocks from the Empire State Building. What sold us on the space was the view—we had an unobstructed vista of the city in every direction; it was spectacular.

On the morning of September 11, I recall coming from a meeting and running into our HR manager, Kerri, who was crying at the elevator. I had no idea what had happened, so Kerri tearfully explained. We all assumed it was a small Cessna that had hit the building, and an accident. However, no one really knew because the phone lines were already down. Everyone crowded into the conference room on the 39th floor to see what was happening, and we all witnessed the second plane crash from the terrorist attacks. We were still watching the surreal scene, holding hands and praying for all the lives lost, when the first tower collapsed. We felt the impact as it rumbled to the ground in a plume of smoke and ash that reached the heavens.

At that point, I feared for our safety; we were the second-tallest building in the neighborhood, after the Empire State Building. We then quickly evacuated, anxiously descending 39 flights of stairs because the elevators were shut down any time there was an emergency. Everyone was concerned for their families, friends, and homes, and we all walked north from the building because there was no transportation. As we walked, we began to encounter people coming from the south, covered in soot and scared to death. While we were walking, we felt the second tower collapse.

This was such a tragic time in New York; we all knew someone who'd been lost. The streets were covered in "Missing" posters and almost everyone cried daily, especially when we'd look to the south and no longer saw the Twin Towers. The towers being gone were a constant reminder of what had happened. People were afraid to go to work, yet we didn't then have work-from-home capability.

Some companies were able to shut down for a while, but we couldn't because every company from around the world needed translation services after the attack. The entire city was traumatized, but we had to be there for our clients—our business didn't stop. I remember we had jobs transcribing the black boxes. (We'd had some prior experience working other plane crashes, which always felt like such a grave responsibility.) As a company, and even though we were scrambling, we threw ourselves into our work and our staff bonded through the collective trauma, all of us braced in case the worst were to happen again.

We didn't focus on major growth in 2001; we instead focused on simply getting through it. We deployed our translation expertise to help fill the needs of a changed world that required our specialized services. It took almost a year for the city to start to feel "normal" again, and even then it was tentative.

And regarding our traditional holiday party? We didn't bring our teams in from around the world that year. Instead, acknowledging the tragedy that was just beginning to heal that cold December of 2001, we felt it was more appropriate to get together in smaller groups in our respective cities. Our NYC team assembled in that 39th-floor conference room for a mellow gathering. We commiserated with one another about lost loved ones, as we looked downtown toward the eerie void in the skyline, at what had been the World Trade Center— and that very rooftop space we had rented in advance a year before.

Post 9/11, like so many other companies, we created a worst-case-scenario guide for how we'd operate during a crisis because what we were doing was so important. Our services were necessary and we had to find ways to become redundant in case the offices ever needed to be evacuated again. After that, we were never without a contingency plan, although Hurricane Sandy in 2012 taught us that sometimes even contingency plans need contingency plans (more on that in Chapter 11).

In business and in life, despite our best efforts, there are times we'll be blindsided by circumstance (I'm looking at you, Hurricane Sandy) and presented with new challenges we never anticipated. Everyone encounters obstacles, but the most successful among us recognize them as opportunities to learn and to grow.

Behind every Traf-O-Data, there may well be a Microsoft; you just have to persevere to get there. So remember the lessons to overcome, which are to be self-reliant, focus on the "can," stay positive, and have a plan.

Maybe make these rhyming lessons into a little song and sing it as loudly as you'd like.

Words of Wisdom

"If at first you don't succeed, you're running about average."

—M.H. Alderson

Building the Business

6

Owning

Ownership is one of my core values and a philosophy every entrepreneur and employee should embrace. As an employee, taking ownership in your job and your company is one of the surest ways you can excel professionally. You position yourself for success when you act as if you own the company, project, or team, regardless of your position or your paygrade.

"Great, Liz," you might say, "but what does creating a culture of ownership mean?"

So glad you asked.

Where Does the Buck Stop? Good Question

Creating a culture of ownership means that no matter where I've been, from Cadet Cleaners to co-CEO of TransPerfect, I've operated with the notion that 100 percent of the company's success was on my shoulders. That means I made myself accountable and held myself responsible for all aspects of what the job entailed. Everywhere I worked, the following questions dictated my behavior:

- How would the owner express gratitude for a customer's business?
- How would the owner process the customer's suggestions?
- How would the owner solve an employee's problem?
- How would the owner encourage teamwork?
- How would the owner communicate an idea?
- How would the owner handle a complaint?
- How would the owner keep abreast of industry changes?
- How would the owner improve service?
- How would the owner innovate?
- How would the owner go the extra mile?
- How does the buck stop with the owner?

Every summer during college, I worked two jobs. My evening and weekend employment was as an usherette for the Toronto Blue Jays because I loved baseball and was able to get paid to watch major league games. Living the dream! But my main job was usually something sales oriented. One year I worked as a telemarketer for *Time* magazine. You know those annoying people who'd interrupt your meal and not take no for an answer, before the advent of caller ID? Yes, that was me.

But I'm not going to apologize, and here's why.

When I called a potential customer to discuss a *Time* magazine subscription, I didn't just see myself as some college kid working a gig where she could sit at a desk from 9 to 5 before standing at the ballpark from 6 to 11; oh, no. In my mind, I was the CEO of Time Warner, Inc., and if I didn't make those sales, the whole company was going to come crashing down, so fictional Art in accounting wouldn't get his pension and imaginary Helen in HR couldn't pay for her mother's bunion surgery. I treated the company like I owned it and like I was accountable to every employee and shareholder.

The telemarketers were given a script, and we weren't supposed to stray from our talking points. However, the script was ridiculous, and the talking points didn't make much sense; they were of no help in selling the subscription. I knew my end goal was to get that subscription, so I would go off script because the prescribed words weren't effective because they sounded like a script. No one wants to be read to on the phone. Fact.

My approach was to have a real conversation with the person who answered the phone. I'd be curious about their life and how they consumed their news, and I'd listen to what they had to say. I knew that if I paid attention, they'd tell me what I needed to know to sell to them. My strategy was to keep them talking, as I found that the more they told me about their lives and the more we developed a relationship, the more likely they were to buy.

The key here was that I believed in the product—and why wouldn't I? I owned the company! I considered ours the most cutting-edge reporting, with articles written by the premier journalists in the industry. What we had to say on those pages was important. I was improving their lives by selling them this portal to knowledge. My pitch was to hit home on all the advantages to the potential subscriber, encouraging them to consider what a small price it was to pay to be so well informed. And because I listened to the potential clients, I was able to customize my pitch because different people have different needs. My approach to the busy homemaker and one to a young executive would be different. (Years later, these skills would be crucial when I was making hundreds of cold calls every day for TransPerfect.)

I was never disciplined for going off script because this technique worked better. Most telemarketing jobs have metrics about numbers of dials and length of time on the phone. I often didn't satisfy those metrics because I'd make fewer dials and speak for longer amounts of time. What was important were my results because of the *quality* of my interactions. No manager's pension was dependent on the number of dials or call length; it was dependent on the number of sales. This was an all-commission position and because I treated it like it was my own, I won the top producer award.

In another job, I worked the position most suitable to any 95-pound co-ed. . .the all-night security guard at my college's computer lab, where I didn't even have the benefit of a knife taped to the wall. However, I knew this was an ideal job because I'd be paid to mind the front desk overnight and I could do my homework or socialize with friends. Because I absolutely believed I could be a security guard and I was the right person for the position, the hiring manager believed it, too. There was no one there to supervise me, so I could have run the lab in any manner I wanted, flagrantly disregarding the rules. But because I acted like I owned the whole damn computer lab while on shift, there was never an issue on my watch.

Words of Wisdom

"Real integrity is doing the right thing, knowing that nobody's going to know whether you did it or not."

—Oprah Winfrey

It's Mine Now

Here's the thing—you don't have to have the job yet to try to take ownership of it. After working an internship in Venezuela after graduation, I stopped in New York to see my sister. She told me about

Euramerica and it sounded like the perfect fit between my desire to work in sales and my passion for languages. I called the company and asked for an interview. Once that was secure, I spoke to them again to see if they had any material I could review prior to my interview. They did, so I immediately went to their office to retrieve it.

I wasn't hired in sales immediately because there were no open positions, so they put me on the production side. That's why I didn't even blink at staying late into the night to see my first project through to the end. My rationale was that the company owner wouldn't have left when there was still work to be done, so I wouldn't either.

The longer I worked at Euramerica, the more I tried to implement the requests and suggestions I heard from both external clients and translators. For example, if Euramerica made a mistake on the client's translation, we'd charge the client for us to fix it. I found this practice unconscionable; it seemed unfair and damaged our relationship with the client. I spent my tenure there coming up with new deliverables and strategies to get sales and production on the same team, instead of working against each other. I attempted to set up production centers by industry and establish pricing guidelines. The problem was that while I ran my job like I owned the company, the company didn't always recognize my ownership, even though they did appreciate my innovation and enthusiasm. No one's ever mad at an employee for trying too hard. (However, an *employee* can absolutely get frustrated by a lack of a career path and just decide to go to grad school instead, before creating that company that *would* implement her ideas....)

When you encourage your employees to take ownership, they become more committed to the organization. Attitudes and productivity improve and creativity is fostered. Workers engage with their jobs and with the company and that synergy can produce amazing results.

Some of the biggest companies now recognize the importance of empowering employees with the notion of ownership. For example, look at the luxury hotelier Ritz-Carlton. At this organization, employees are encouraged to find opportunities to improve the guest's experience during their stay, with the parameter of spending up to $2,000 per guest without having to seek authorization. This isn't even necessarily about placating unhappy vacationers; rather, it's about enhancing their visit to a property.

Five-Star Staff

In an article for *Forbes*, Micah Solomon described an experience where a guest's son lost his Thomas the Tank Engine toy somewhere on the Dove Mountain Resort in Arizona. The toy was particularly special to the child. The mother explained how devastated her boy would be if the toy could not be located. The staff couldn't find the child's tank engine, but they were determined to create a positive outcome. They went to the toy store and found a duplicate Thomas train. Had they simply sent that along, it surely would have been enough.

But no.

Solomon writes, "[The staff] composed a note in longhand to the boy—in the voice of Thomas the Tank Engine himself—telling a sweet tale about the extended vacation Thomas had taken after being accidentally left behind. The account included adorable pictures of Thomas exploring the property, cooking in the Ritz-Carlton kitchen, and more. Four days after the disappearance of Thomas, he arrived by mail to a family that was, understandably, blown away, and that has shared the story at every chance they can find on Facebook and elsewhere, proclaiming that 'The Ritz has earned our business for years to come!'"[1]

Just the Facts

Seventy-one percent of executives say that employee engagement is critical to their company's success, and companies with a highly engaged workforce are 21 percent more profitable.[2]

Per Natalie Lambert in the *Huffington Post*, "What enterprises want is the kind of employee engagement that stems from feeling empowered at work. These employees are sixty-seven percent more willing to put in extra effort on the job. They're also more willing to innovate and take the creative risks that help drive business growth and revenue gains."[3]

Another company that sets the gold standard for employee empowerment is Chewy.com, an online pet supply store. Recently, when a customer contacted their service line to see if she could return an unopened bag of auto-shipped food because her dog had passed away, Chewy went above and beyond. They instructed the bereaved buyer to simply donate the food to a shelter and they'd issue a refund, but they also sent her flowers and a sweet note because of her loss. The customer was so moved by the kindness and sensitivity of the customer service rep that she tweeted about her experience. That one tweet not only garnered hundreds of thousands of retweets, but also caused thousands of testimonials to pour in from other satisfied Chewy customers.[4] This is the impact that a single empowered employee can make on the bottom line.

We found the notion of empowerment to be so important that we made innovation a requirement for promotion to many positions. To get to the next level, employees had to come up with a new product, service, or practice. The desire for innovation was as an integral part of the corporate culture as an air hockey table was to companies at the dawn of the dot-com era. However, we didn't put the onus for creating entirely on the staff; instead, management helped them with surveys and contests meant to get them thinking about what they would do if they owned the company.

Whose House? Our House

Tim Cook, CEO of Apple, discussed the concept of creating an innovation culture in an interview with the dean of Duke's Fuqua School of Business, saying, "You look for people that are not political; people who are not bureaucrats; people who really don't care who gets the credit. People that can privately celebrate the achievement but not care if their name's the one in the lights....You look for wicked smart people. You look for people who appreciate different points of view. You look for people who care enough that they have an idea at 11 pm at night and they want to call and talk to you about it. Because they are so excited about it and they want to push the idea further. And they believe that somebody can help them push the idea another step instead of them doing everything."[5]

For many years, I interviewed every single new hire. One of my favorite questions was to ask that if they were working in an ice cream shop, how would they deal with a situation where they caught a coworker stealing from the cash register. I wanted to know what they'd do as: (1) the coworker, (2) the manager, and (3) the owner. The answer I wanted entailed that employee treating the ice cream shop like it was their own and stopping the thief as their first order of business. I wanted the owner to fire that person and I wanted the manager to fire that person. And while I'd have been impressed if the coworker tried to fire that person (way to take ownership!), I would have been satisfied if they made them put the money back and told the manager. Think about it—the owner wouldn't wait to speak to that employee's manager; they'd slap that person's hand out of the till and give them their marching orders. That was the expectation I had for workers at each level.

While I appreciated those potential hires who looked at this exercise more thoughtfully, wondering if the sticky-fingered employee might be experiencing duress in their personal life, I wasn't hiring anyone who'd try to morally equivocate, justifying the theft. I was in the translation business, not social work.

The reason I started asking this question is that I had an experience with a production person we'll call Stefan, who worked directly with the vendors, in this case a typesetting company. In Stefan's mind, net profit for our company was not a priority. He took it upon himself to intervene, but not in a way that might have been useful to management. He never sat down and stated his case, an action that would have impressed me. He never approached me with facts and figures about vendor satisfaction. He didn't present me with a problem that I could have, if not solved, then at least helped him understand how important profit was to growth and the overall success of the organization.

Instead of the legitimate steps to take ownership, he took a shortcut.

Stefan asked the accounting team to give him the vendor's pay envelope before it went out. It turned out he had inserted a note suggesting that the company charge TransPerfect more, even though we were paying them a competitive rate. In this case, it could be argued that he was treating our company like he owned it, but the strategy only works when operating in an ethical and loyal manner, and one that moves the company forward. To this day, I don't understand his motivations, but yes, I fired him, like so many disloyal ice cream shop thieves.

As my career progressed, and I learned from my own experience, I honed the questions I'd ask myself regarding ownership:

- How would the owner ensure the highest quality?
- How would the owner spoil the clients with superior service?
- How would the owner anticipate what the client needed before the client knew they needed it?
- How would the owner introduce new products and service ideas?
- How would the owner create a company that is the employer of choice in its industry and, ideally, any industry?
- How would the owner make it so clients never want to leave and employees never want to quit?
- How would the owner provide the best training in the industry?
- How would the owner instill the importance of loyalty to the company?
- How would the owner create a culture of everyone treating the company's money like their own?
- How would the owner align company and employee incentives and create systems so a Stefan situation never happened again?

Ownership should be everyone's responsibility within the organization, and particularly with mid-level managers. For example, say you're a middle manager at a factory and the people on your line aren't happy with something the company is doing. Maybe the tools are outdated, or perhaps the workload is too heavy. Or maybe you're the shift manager at the ice cream shop and there's an issue with the flavor of the chocolate chip—the quality of the chocolate is low and it tastes waxy and that's impacting the employees' tips and the customers' loyalty.

Listening to and empathizing with the employees is not enough; that mid-level boss must take these concerns to senior management. That manager must try to work out what's right offline, rather than just nodding and saying, "I know the ice cream recipe sucks, but having it taste like a chewy candle is just the way it is." Senior management can't fix a problem they don't know exists and that mid-level manager is doing the company a disservice by not bringing it to their attention. These bosses must act like owners, being conduits among all levels. If the employees love their boss but despise "senior management" or "the company," the manager is probably not doing their job. (Of course, there have been well-documented times this approach hasn't worked, like when middle management raised issues about the Boeing 737 MAX and upper management turned a blind eye, but this circumstance is an outlier.)

Even if that mid-level boss can't get the problem fixed, it's imperative that this person sit down with leadership to get to the whys behind what's amiss. If the boss can go back to the employees and explain how, say, a meddlesome bit of gear is an OSHA requirement, then the rules won't feel as random or capricious to those they impact. Listening to employees will make them more receptive to bringing new ideas, especially when they see that some of them will be implemented, creating that wanted culture of innovation. For example, one of our employees suggested to me that we develop our own certification for our translators. It was a terrific idea. We implemented it, called it TLC (TransPerfect Linguist Certification), and eventually our team came up with 80 different tests for languages in 12 different fields, which at the time created the gold standard for quality in the translation industry.

The Hap-Hap-Happiest Christmas

I can point to our success as being a result of the culture of ownership. **This growth can be directly linked to everyone taking ownership**, whether it was dropping off a completed project at 2 a.m. or working 24/7. Our team acted like owners because we didn't have them doing anything we founders weren't doing ourselves. (I refer you again to our employee who wouldn't take out the trash.) No matter the size of the job, we'd take the project, even when it meant adjusting the staffing to accommodate the impossible—translating a million words per month. What was so rewarding for me was to see these recent college grads we'd hired eventually managing hundreds of people, becoming millionaires in their own right. Our team also acted like owners because we hired incredibly motivated and entrepreneurial individuals and aligned their compensation and position with their results.

Years before, we'd set the precedent of taking ownership by doing what other companies wouldn't do. After a couple of years of 100-hour weeks, I was set to take my first vacation over the Christmas holidays, departing on Christmas Eve. The dream of a cozy Christmas in picturesque Vermont was what I'd visualize when I needed to push past my limitations. My suitcase was packed with my fuzzy sweater, cozy socks, and woolly hat. I was so ready to be done for the year, ensconced in a charming, snow-blanketed town straight out of a non-problematic Hallmark movie.

We were practically locking the door to the office when the phone rang. Goldman Sachs was calling. They had an important project that had to be completed over the holidays. We'd only done a few projects with Goldman before, although over the past year, we'd sent hundreds of pitch letters to everyone in their corporate directory. They told us their primary translation service was closed and could we accommodate them? I took this request so personally. I thought to myself, *You mean, could I change my plans and do work for the company that dinged me when I was interviewing with them after grad school, and finally have a chance to prove my worth to them?*

This situation reminded me of a time in high school, once my leg was healed. My parents would send my sister and me north every weekend to ski with the Raven Ski Club. One morning, we were in the middle of a horrendous snowstorm. The bus to the mountain was only a quarter full, because so many people shied away due to the weather. But there was an end-of-the-season race and I was determined to compete in it, despite the conditions. I wanted to prove myself. Not only did I complete, but I ended up winning the race. This helped me realize that **if we just show up when others don't and outwork everyone else, we can accomplish great things in this world.**

My answer to Goldman Sachs was the same as the day my sister and I had chosen to get on the bus: "Absolutely, we're on our way."

A caveat here is that my partner and I were young, and a couple, and had no other responsibilities outside of work, so we were willing to make the sacrifice. This is why I believe that it's easier to start a company when you're young, because you don't have all the obligations that come with time as you get older.

We worked straight through Christmas Day, spending the night in the Goldman office, missing presents and family sing-alongs. (Perhaps this part was for the best.) We did not hang our stockings with care by the Bloomberg terminals, although we were tempted. I traded the idea of a bucolic family holiday for the present, which was the loyalty and trust of a marquee client that helped us grow our business exponentially.

Even Santa Claus was willing to wait to win Goldman's business.

So, whether it's your hobby or your life's work, taking ownership is one of the most expedient ways to position yourself for success.

The buck stops with you.

Words of Wisdom

"Hard work spotlights the character of people: some turn up their sleeves, some turn up their noses, and some don't turn up at all."

—Sam Ewing

7

Balancing

Balance is one of those skills that looks so easy to the casual observer. Watch an Olympic gymnast compete on the beam—they perform on it like it's four feet wide. But it's actually four inches wide, the same width as a Coronavirus vaccination card.[1] That's why balance is tricky; it looks so easy when you don't know the effort that goes into achieving it.

Balance for Beginners

I used to think I was fantastic at balance, particularly when I was in college. As important as my studies were, I made sure that I had a fulfilling social life. In college, my goals were good grades, fun, and enough money in my pocket not to feel stressed all the time, and that required striking a balance. I learned to maximize my time by prioritizing; if I had schoolwork to do, that was done first because I knew I couldn't relax and enjoy myself until I finished my work. Procrastination has always stressed me out, and I can't put forth my best work when I feel pressured.

I loved a good gathering and was fortunate to go to Trinity College, a school with both incredible academics and countless parties. I was able to go out five nights a week and, often, two parties a night. I loved my social life in college, and it went a long way toward making up for tenth grade.

Some people thrive under a pending deadline, truly pulling it together when in a pinch; they're called *lunatics*, and I am not one of them. Every morning when I'd wake up, I'd create a plan for my day, knowing that if I accomplished it all, I could go to a party or event that night. I can think of plenty of parties and sporting events where I may have missed the beginning or the first quarter or inning. However, I was more afraid of failure than of missing out, so I had the discipline to stay home until I'd finished my assignment. I looked at classes and part-time jobs as the price I had to pay to earn my fun.

After college and my time in Venezuela, I started at Euramerica, and I loved everything about the company's culture. So many of my coworkers were my age, and we shared a work hard/play hard philosophy. During this time, I met a cute young attorney named Mike and we began dating. Mike and I were a fantastic team, but we weren't ready for a more serious commitment; he was moving to Los Angeles for a job opportunity and I was staying in New York for B-school.

My strategy for balancing work and social time followed me to Stern, where I always made sure to go to the weekly Thursday night beer blasts because they were my favorite times. I also loved living in New York, taking advantage of all the city had to offer, as well as spending time with my friends. Life was good. I had the opportunity to get an apartment with some friends during my second year of B-school, but I demurred and stayed in my Tudor City studio because I thought I'd lack the willpower to put my studies first if the party were happening in my own home. I needed complete silence and isolation to get into the zone.

I gave no thought to the notion of balance after starting TransPerfect, and that was an intentional gamble. I'd rolled the dice that **if I worked today like no one else would, I could live tomorrow like no one else could.** Because my co-CEO was my then-boyfriend whom I'd met in B-school, my business and personal life were utterly entwined, at least until we stopped dating a few years later. Even then, 100 percent of my time was focused on growing the company. Again, it never felt like work because I was around such fun, motivated people with shared goals. No one's watching the clock when your job entails singing Bon Jovi songs with employees at a karaoke bar. Years into my time at TransPerfect and after Phil and I had broken up, I had the good fortune to reconnect with Mike. We were both older and more established in our careers, and suddenly the idea of getting more serious was both timely and thrilling. While I loved my life and my career, I realized that he was the missing piece.

So, 11 short years after we'd first met, Mike and I were married in Jamaica, and I started balancing marriage with the company. For six months after we got married, we lived on opposite coasts, traveling cross-country to see each other. When I was out there, I worked in our LA office during the day and we were together at night. In this case, balance looked like compartmentalization.

Suffice it to say, I thought I knew how to balance multiple things, until motherhood hit me like a screeching halt. Being a working mom taught me that I couldn't do it all at the same time. At this stage, we had approximately 150 employees, around $20 million in revenue, and about a dozen offices. The company still needed my full-time attention.

When I'm interviewed about being a female entrepreneur, I'm often asked about how I maintained a work-life balance once I had my children. (Exactly the same kind of questions everyone asks Warren Buffett and Jamie Dimon, *ahem*.)

The short answer, and one that I hope is the case for fewer and fewer working women is, I didn't.

Keeping the Balls in the Air

Balance implies a sense of equilibrium, where all sides are given equal weight and prioritization, and that was not the case with me, at least in the beginning. **Being a working, engaged parent is less about balancing and more about juggling, a desperate attempt to keep all the moving pieces from crashing to the floor.** When you have so many balls in the air, you have to recognize which ones are glass, because you don't want them to break. Traditionally, this was a more common dilemma for working mothers, but as times change and we progress, this applies to all parents.

Mike and I had our first son in November 2000. I was the first person in the company to have a baby, so we didn't have any protocols in place. I went to work on a Wednesday, walked to the hospital that afternoon, and gave birth that same night. I stayed in the hospital until Friday and returned to work on Monday. Let me say that again: I was able to *take the weekend off* to have a baby. And that's it. My desire to just hold my baby in my arms and marvel at him, with his porcelain skin and delicate wisps of hair, was overwhelming. (Circumstances I'll get into later prevented me from taking any more time.) The physical toll the birth had on my body and the exhaustion and hormones raging through my system—none of that was allowed to take precedence over the job I had to do.

Does this sound outrageous when you read this? Because it felt outrageous when I lived it.

I learned a valuable lesson about succession planning. When running your company, you should always have a second-in-command for every position, including your own, someone trusted and competent who can take over if the need arises and on a moment's notice. Succession planning is important to any firm because you never know what will pull your employees away, whether it's parental leave, taking a new job, or the proverbial getting hit by a bus.

At least I was fortunate to be in the position to have a support system in place for my son with a fantastic, connected father who was also building his own career and an amazing full-time babysitter, a privilege that's not tenable for many working women. At that age, babies need a warm body to feed them and change their diapers, so it wasn't as imperative that I be with them every minute. It's only because I knew he'd be loved and cared for that I was able to keep tending to my first, nonhuman baby—the one that supported dozens of families and facilitated communications around the world.

What kept me going was knowing that if I tended to the shop now, I'd be there when my son—and later two sons—was older. That's when children need their parents most, because bigger kids mean bigger problems. My philosophy was that by the time they were teens and desperate for my counsel, I'd have paid my dues.

When we had our second son in 2003, it wasn't any better. I worked a full day on Friday, had my baby on Saturday (which was my birthday), and was back at work on Monday. It was almost a joke at this point, like, "What'd you do this weekend, Liz?" "Had another baby." Again, this schedule was not my choice. When I'd read history books about women working the fields, giving birth, and getting right back to their task at hand, it never occurred to me I would be in a similar situation.

In a perfect world, I'd have had maternity leave, but I couldn't because I had too much responsibility and no backup. My partner and I had segmented our roles and there were tasks only I was doing, such as signing checks and overseeing payroll. If I wasn't in the office, doing my job, our employees, subcontractors, and vendors didn't get paid. I couldn't even work much from home because at that time the hardware and connectivity weren't what they are now.

So, in the beginning, I had all the stress of a newborn baby, plus all the demands of being a co-CEO. My days consisted of being in the office and managing crises while using my Medela pump at 7 a.m.,

11 a.m., 3 p.m., 7 p.m., and 11 p.m. My pump was as ubiquitous as my purse and my exhaustion and the guilt that I wasn't giving enough to my baby or my company.

When I'd arrive back at my apartment in those early days, I'd nurse for hours. I loved the bonding time, but because of reflux, after an hour of nursing they would often throw up, and I'd need to start the process all over again. I cried every day and I never slept.

I had no balance.

Again, I felt like I had no choice. The only thing I could manage in this situation was to make it work. While our children are the silver lining, we working moms should be so impressed by what we can accomplish under such duress. (Personally, I was surprised at how productive I was when I was up all night answering emails while nursing.)

Just the Facts

For every child a woman has, she makes 4 percent less. Men, on the other hand, make 6 percent more.[2]

At the time I was a part of Young Presidents' Organization, a group of CEOs whose companies had revenue of at least $8 million and over 50 employees. There were 13 of us in my monthly forum group, and I was the only woman. I thought it was important personally and professionally to network and learn from those who were in similar situations. As it turns out, none of the men faced the same struggles that I did, and not just because they weren't founders, or worked for larger organizations. The issue was that they didn't feel so torn between their work and home life; they didn't have to make the same either/or choices that I did as a mother.

Not long after I had my children, I recall sitting in the room listening to these guys drone on about strategy, and I realized I'd much rather be with my boys than stuck in a meeting, so I quit the group.

It was liberating.

Desperately Seeking Equilibrium

I needed to find balance, which was far more of a challenge than I'd ever imagined. There was a clear line dividing the moms who worked outside the home and those who didn't. Instead, I often felt as though I'd joined the wrong sorority and was to be pitied.

When my children went to preschool, the stay-at-home mothers came to drop-off wearing exercise clothing. They always looked so casual and relaxed and happy. They were all the best of friends and they'd hang out and have coffee afterwards, while I rushed off to meetings in my business clothing. "Oh, my goodness, are you scurrying off to the office again, Liz?" I remember being asked. Even though I wore power suits and Italian heels, somehow I still felt like that kid who showed up to high school with a giant cast and a platform saddle shoe.

I wasn't one of *them*.

I wasn't able to take on roles like that of class parent, although I went on all the field trips I could and tried to hit every extracurricular activity possible.

I often couldn't shake the feeling of guilt that I should be wherever I wasn't. I ached for my children when I wasn't with them, and I worried about the company when I was off on an excursion with the boys. I was perpetually torn, trying to be the best mother and CEO. One year, our family took a ski trip in the Poconos for my and my son's birthday, and after a day on the slopes being there and present, I spent the night sitting on the floor of our hotel room bathroom, exhausted, responding to work emails and making calls. This wasn't an isolated incident. My son still reminds me of these trips, saying that I spent all night in the bathroom.

When I needed to travel for business or an international sales conference, I'd arrive at the last possible minute and leave the moment the meetings ended, in order to get home to my family.

My schedule was relentless, and my focus was so pulled in every direction that I worried that I was perpetually disappointing everyone. It's not that I didn't love everything I was doing, it's just that I always felt torn.

Words of Wisdom

"I think that if you love what you do, and the choice you've made in your life, somehow that drives you forward to enjoy it all. Even in the chaos, even in the exhaustion of it, and even when it seems out of balance."

—Angelina Jolie

Later, when my kids went to elementary school, I befriended a couple of moms who had high-powered careers. The social life I'd had prior to children was almost entirely TransPerfect-based, but once I had children, I was excited to connect with women in similar situations. My mom friends and I would walk together to work after drop-off, with each of us peeling off as we walked south to our respective offices. It felt good to have a small community of women who understood how it felt to be so fragmented, and so judged by those who'd made different choices and didn't respect mine.

I always did early morning breakfast and drop-off because it was more precious time that I had with the boys. For a while, a group of mothers in the neighborhood did drop-offs for each other. I'll never forget the day that I had an emergency and I asked one nonworking mother if it would be okay just this once for my babysitter to do the group drop-off instead. Her response still chills me to this day. *"I did not quit my job so my children could be catered to by the help."*

Words of Wisdom

"I think that while all mothers deal with guilt, working mothers are plagued by guilt on steroids."

—Arianna Huffington

Lessons from the Fall

Mine was not a circumstance I would wish on anyone, but it taught me a couple of lessons.

First, to be a working mother, I learned that I had to compartmentalize like I used to do back in school. I realized that I was setting a poor example by being the boss and sending emails at all hours because that set the expectation that everyone should do the same. Eventually I figured out **that I would never get past the guilt of not being in two places at once, but I could mitigate it by being fully present wherever I was.** That meant leaving the office at 6 p.m. sharp, and not spending the rest of my family time looking at my phone. Then, once the kids were asleep around 10:30 p.m., I'd get back on email for a few hours before bed. I know that finding balance is hard, but it will be easier if you (and hopefully, your company) make it about results instead of hours, which I recommend across the board at all times.

So many women go the route that I did, choosing to work and pump and never sleep. According to the Bureau of Labor Statistics, 71 percent of mothers with children in the home are working.[3] **I worked with some of those women and I salute them all because it's incredibly difficult.**

Another of the many ideas our employees introduced came from Maria Simon and Jennifer LeCates, two of our terrific salespeople, which was creating our Women's Group. Many of our women leaders were embarking on having a family, so this group was needed. The goal was to support and retain them, encouraging their continued growth at the company through motherhood. I regret not doing this sooner and expanding on how we offered it so more women throughout the company could benefit from it. On top of this, it's important to set up family policies not just for women, but also for men.

However, your remaining on the job may well be worth it, especially when it comes to creating gender equality. Per Kathleen L. McGinn of the Harvard Business School, girls who were raised by working women grow up more likely to have a supervisory role on the job. In an article for *HBS*, she says, "There's a lot of parental guilt about having both parents working outside the home. But what this research says to us is that not only are you helping your family economically—and helping yourself professionally and emotionally if you have a job you love—but you're also helping your kids. So, I think for both mothers and for fathers, working both inside and outside the home gives your kids a signal that contributions at home and at work are equally valuable, for both men and women. In short, it's good for your kids."[4]

If you choose to stay home after having children, I understand the draw. I can't even explain how many times I wanted to be the cute mom with the green juice and the pack of friends heading to breakfast. Some women dream of Brad Pitt, but my fantasies involved athleisure wear and pancakes. Still, my advice is to keep one foot in your industry to stay relevant. Perhaps it means taking the occasional consulting gig or working one day a week. Enroll in an online class or maintain your credentials. Maybe do some volunteer work for a nonprofit—anything you can do to keep up your skills.

Whatever you do, please don't completely quit because it's too hard to get back in after a long absence. We're already seeing the impact of this now with women who were furloughed during Covid. As I wrote in an article for *Forbes*, "In the last year, more than 2.3 million women left the American workforce, reaching our lowest participation levels since the end of the Reagan administration. That's over *thirty years* of gains wiped out in less than one. Many will not return. And many who do will find themselves facing a greater mountain to scale with a whole lot less footing."[5] Do what you can to stay current, because you never know what the future holds.

I'd be remiss if I didn't mention that now is the perfect time to start your own company if you want to attain balance and create the ideal corporate culture by running the show yourself. First, it's easier than ever with all the tools available for building a presence on the internet. Second, social media can help you market and promote cost-effectively and efficiently on a global scale. In an article for CNBC, I explained, "I think the best solution for women ultimately is entrepreneurship. If women can start their own companies, or in partnership with other women, that can allow a degree of financial independence or flexibility."[6]

Above all, what I learned from my own experience is how important it is to run or work for a company that has a good plan in place for families. As it currently stands, research shows that the longer a woman's maternity leave is, the higher the perception is that the woman isn't committed to her career, particularly unfortunate because longer maternity leaves are linked to lower infant mortality and reduced maternal stress.[7] The harsh truth is that women who take longer leaves are less likely to receive promotions, raises, and new opportunities, and are more likely to face a demotion, firing, or a layoff—and this is a choice so many of us have had to face. This flies in the face of the notion of creating work-life balance. That's why I'm a fierce advocate for protecting women's jobs when they have children because I understand how important it is not to lose that talent. Protecting women under Title VII (allowing 12 weeks of unpaid leave) is not enough.

Just the Facts

Researchers at London's South Bank University found that almost 50 percent of the women surveyed discovered that taking maternity leave negatively impacted their careers.[8]

When you compare what US law mandates versus a country like Sweden, there is no comparison. The Swedes believe strongly in gender equality, having enacted parental leave for both sexes in 1974. Now, parents are given a total of 480 days of paid leave in cases of both birth and adoption, and a single parent is entitled to take all 480 days. Other countries are far more progressive as well. For example, in Lithuania, women get 70 days prior to birth and almost two months after at full salary and Canadians can get 55 percent of their pay for a 17-week leave, and then take another 35 weeks unpaid.[9]

If there's any good news to be had here, some US companies are stepping up to better support new parents. For example, Etsy offers 26 weeks of parental leave for birth or adoption, and they allow the parents to spread this leave out over two years so it best accommodates the new family.

Balance with Benefits for Working Women

Ultimately, it behooves employers to help working women find balance. And we need women in the workplace because everyone benefits from having more than just one perspective. For example, in 1983 when the engineers at NASA were planning to send Sally Ride to space for six days, they inquired if 100 tampons would be the proper number to send with her. The staff, presumably all male (and possibly having never met a woman), had to ask because she was the first female American to go to space. When interviewed about this situation years later, Ride said, "There were probably some other, similar sorts of issues, just because they had never thought about what kind of personal equipment a female astronaut would take."[10] I use this example because for most of history and as demonstrated by the NASA engineers, women didn't have a significant role in the workplace, to everyone's detriment.

Fortunately, times are changing for women in the workforce and nowhere is this more evident than at the Diva corporation, which I discussed in a *Forbes* interview with its founder, Carinne Chambers-Saini. She said, "We introduced Paid Menstrual Leave last year, in part to help destigmatize periods in the workplace—in our own workplace. Eligible staff are entitled to one paid day off per month so they can take care of themselves on the worst days of their period. This ensures them that they have space and time to tend to their bodies and return to work feeling ready to face the day. Based on a recent survey, we know that the vast majority of Diva staff are comfortable with taking their menstrual leave—many people even update their Slack status to the blood droplet to let their colleagues know why they're not at their desk."[11]

It's so nice to see that companies are beginning to make accommodations for every employee, because that will go a long way in helping working mothers find balance. And I eventually did get to take my "maternity leave," almost 20 years later.

But that's a story for another chapter.

8

Competing

Y ou may have the greatest product or service in the world, but without being able to sell it, you won't have a company for long. So in this chapter, we're going to talk about not only how the sausage is made but also how it is sold in a crowded marketplace.

Words of Wisdom

"The healthiest competition occurs when average people win by putting above average effort."

—Colin Powell

How Do You Like Them Apples?

Our first concern with our nascent company was figuring out how we'd differentiate ourselves from the competition. To the uninitiated, translation services can seem like a commodity, especially given the overlap of translators working for more than one employer. If we'd adopted the attitude that we were all doing the same sort of work for the same client base—an apples-to-apples comparison—the natural inclination would be to sell on price.

That would have been a mistake.

The nature of business is that you will always have competition; it's inevitable. However, if you're somehow the only player in the game and you've cornered the market, my advice is don't get too comfortable because it won't last. If you're experiencing any sort of success, I guarantee another company is going to come along with a slightly different way of doing what you do. (Try not to look surprised when it happens.) **New businesses are often less about inventing something so much as finding a differentiator in an established market.**

Let's say you've created the world's most effective widget, and it solves every problem effortlessly. Yours is the last widget anyone ever needs to buy. . .until someone new makes it in blue. Look at ride-share companies Uber and Lyft. Uber was first and then Lyft came along and did the exact same thing, only with a pink mustache on the car's grill. (Basically, they made the widget blue.)

Even now, the same gig workers often work for both companies, driving their same personal vehicle, picking up the same customers. However, since each company's inception, there are enough discernible differences that passengers tend to choose one or the other because the organizations are unique. For example, Lyft offered the option for drivers to receive tips on day one, whereas it took years for Uber to roll out this option.

Per author Alex Rosenblat, "It's not uncommon for drivers to describe Uber passengers as higher class but also as stuck up, and to say they prefer Lyft because the passengers are more friendly or engaging."[1] Lyft drivers have the perception of being "a friend with a car," whereas Uber tries to come across as more of a black car service. Again, even though it's common to see drivers with both Lyft and Uber branding on their cars and two different cell phones sitting in their cup holders, this highlights that there are key differences in both client and corporate cultures. To better compete for clients and contractors, Lyft and Uber had to understand how they differed and position themselves accordingly.

Per Lora Kolodny in a CNBC article, "Uber's ambitions are 'horizontal,' going beyond ride-hailing into food delivery, freight, air taxis and driverless car technology. Lyft's are 'vertical,' focused on transportation."[2] So, what seems like an apples-to-apples comparison at first glance, especially given a shared contractor and vehicle pool, is really the difference between baking an apple pie with a soft, buttery Golden Delicious versus a tart, bitter Granny Smith. They're both apples, but that's where the similarities end. (If you're not a baker, please note that the former is perfection and the other will get you mocked at Thanksgiving dessert.)

Let's talk about another similar example—Coke versus Pepsi. Again, on the surface, their business models and consumers seem quite similar, as do their titular products. When poured into a clear glass, the brown, effervescent liquid is indistinguishable.

It's only once you delve into how each company operates that their differences become evident.

For example, PepsiCo has a far more diverse product portfolio. They're more than just a beverage company; they own brands like Ruffles, Lays, Doritos, and Cheetos. Only 46 percent of their revenue comes from beverage sales.[3] And PepsiCo prices its products based on consumer demand and demographics, whereas Coca-Cola prices its products based on how their competition is priced.[4] These are two wildly divergent approaches. While the variations between the companies might not seem any greater than a vanilla-raisin versus a citrus aftertaste to the average consumer, the way each entity does business is entirely different.

So if you're ever in a restaurant and you tell the waitstaff you'll have "Coke or Pepsi, whatever, it's the same thing," please know a soda executive just died a little inside.

In positioning our company, I knew we'd be up against plenty of two-person shops, also run from someone's kitchen table in the early days. We'd likely work with the same translators and we'd be fighting for some of the same clients, a real Uber/Lyft conundrum. We had to find a way to differentiate ourselves. We needed to prove why *our* apples would make the best pie, so our job was to discern where we could separate ourselves from the pack and play to those strengths. I knew we could be competitive with pricing initially as we didn't have much overhead. However, I didn't want to set us up as a shop that sold on price because that's not sustainable; I wanted to win business on service and value-add, two traits I saw lacking in the industry.

I knew the market from my previous experience. While all of our potential clients were conscious of pricing, fees were rarely the sole deciding factor and that's often the case. Take BMW, for example. There are a lot of fine automobiles out there, and some that offer superior performance, but BMW is a brand that sets itself apart by giving every buyer or lessee their Ultimate Care plan. This plan includes oil changes and all scheduled maintenance as part of the lease or sale for the first 36,000 miles. While the vehicles receive their free servicing, owners can relax in a lounge with coffee and Wi-Fi (sometimes donuts, depending on the dealer), or they're given loaners. Does taking care of what can be a pesky but necessary task make a car cost more? Yes. Does this also help BMW maintain higher satisfaction ratings than the industry average? Also yes. (Probably even more so if every dealership offered donuts.)

From my time at Euramerica, I knew that clients clamored for the highest quality and service, and I knew if we could satisfy these needs, we could charge more for our services. Our initial differentiator would be our sense of urgency, a trait our competitors lacked. One of my biggest frustrations when I was at Euramerica was that it took far too long to provide a quote or turn around a job. Because I knew this was an issue, I made sure we delivered proposals and projects quickly. Speedier service is the same reason Amazon Prime memberships are so popular. That's why 200 million people are willing to fork over a small premium to get what they need sooner.[5]

Just the Facts

Regarding accelerated shipping times, 65 percent of consumers reveal they would be willing to pay more for faster, more reliable e-commerce services.[6]

To make the business a contender, we'd provide personalized service, spoiling the clients. We always had a live person answering the phone, rather than a recording, because we believed in the personal touch. Instead of balking at rush jobs, we'd accommodate them. We used to send our clients containers of chocolates. We included a note with the container that whenever they wanted more, to give us a call and we'd come over to fill it up because it prompted them to interact with us. While candy wasn't exactly golfing at Pebble Beach— something we'd eventually do—this was a way to make sure our company's name stayed on our clients' lips (and possibly hips). In the very early days, we brought our contact from Cyprus Minerals into town, putting her up in a hotel and taking her to a Broadway show. The expense was a stretch for us, but we wanted to show her exactly how much we appreciated her business, because Cyprus was the company that got us out of the dorm room and into an office.

Words of Wisdom

"Good service means never having to ask for anything."

—Danny Meyer

Our plan was to set ourselves apart with our creativity, customizing products and services. We'd proactively anticipate what the clients might need, expending on the deliverables to offer a full range of services over what competitors could provide. The philosophy was that when a client needed a project translated in a hurry, cost became even less of a consideration. They knew they could count on us to get the job done, because we wouldn't hesitate to hire shifts of translators working 24/7 or enlist 200 of them for a time-sensitive million-word project.

In always communicating with our clients, we'd eventually uncover needs we could fulfill to make ours a one-stop shop, much in the same way that grocery stores started adding bank or pharmacy branches inside of them, or how the good Target in town will have a Starbucks. While selling coffee was never Target's core business, studies have recently shown that drinking a caffeinated coffee while shopping causes consumers to purchase more impulse items and spend more overall in the store.[7] Yet the idea likely came from Target asking their guests what could improve their shopping experience.

We worked with the Global 200, meaning the 200 largest law firms in the world. For an example of how we expanded our offerings, we started a litigation support services arm. We formed this because as we fulfilled translation requests during mergers and acquisitions, one of our senior sales leaders uncovered a host of other services we could offer, including copying, scanning, coding, and blow-backs (putting digitized or recorded content onto paper). Later, this evolved into being able to offer e-discovery, deposition services, and legal staffing solutions, including providing attorneys. Again, while these services weren't our core business, they supplemented it. This is how we turned small accounts into $20 million behemoths, one Xerox at a time.

In the early days, we focused on offering the highest quality of translation services with the quickest turnaround times. That way, we could bring in business we would not otherwise get and charge more. Eventually, because of service, quality, and innovation, ours became the marquee brand in the space. That's when we truly rolled out the VIP treatment for clients with trips to places like Napa and Cannes and San Sebastián. One of my favorite perks was when we offered a Women's Retreat at Miraval in Arizona, where our senior female clients came for a resort and spa weekend with empowerment seminars.

Events like these helped us truly get to know our clients. I wholeheartedly agree with Harvey Mackay, author of *Swim with the Sharks Without Being Eaten Alive*, who suggested going through a 60-question survey about your clients, finding out about their interests, activities, and families. This will allow you to develop real friendships with them. Establishing those relationships will help you deliver that personal touch, like knowing to send a birthday bottle of Japanese whisky to a client who is a connoisseur. The bonus here is that in the rare instance when you make a mistake or have an issue, your clients are far more likely to be understanding and extend grace.

When you're doing business with a company that treats you like royalty and provides a superior work product, why would you even consider going elsewhere to save a few dollars?

They're Good; We're Great

I've never crafted a sales pitch based on what's wrong with the other guys; denigrating the competition is for amateurs. **Not smack-talking your competitors is particularly important if you spend your career selling in the same industry, working for various companies.** The average tenure at a company is 4.1 years, and the most successful people move on anywhere from two to five years.[8] This means there's a good chance you'll end up in front of some of the same clients and you'll impair your credibility when suddenly you're touting a service that you previously bashed.

A far better way to sell and compete is to gain a solid understanding of what your client needs. My mentor Jack Daly used to say, "Don't show up and throw up," because if you spend the whole time telling a potential customer why your company is so great, you won't be paying attention to the cues they're giving you. While you're busy expounding on, say, exactly how fast you are, that decision-maker may be reminded of the huge mess created when the last vendor went too quickly and delivered error-riddled results. No one lives down translating a prospectus where the company describes their initial *pubic* offering. (If you think your coworkers won't write that in icing on your retirement cake 30 years later, think again.)

My philosophy was to sell on the customized approach; if a company needed to work in 10 countries with a local presence, we had them covered. If they were producing information in an ISO-certified industry, we were the right partner because we were ISO-certified. Rush services, staffing, or specific legal expertise? We would create a plan to serve them. Take the example of JCPenney, our first million-dollar account. Their headquarters was in Plano, Texas, so we opened a Dallas office to better serve them. And that's another reason to make sure you're listening to your potential clients—they'll guide you toward services you should be offering if you aren't already. . .like being able to get a pumpkin spice latte at Target.

Words of Wisdom

"I like to listen. I have learned a great deal from listening carefully. Most people never listen."

—Ernest Hemingway

Is It on Sale?

Eventually the language services space became more commoditized and pricing started to come down, due in part to new competitors, more sophisticated computer-aided translation (CAT) tools that aided in translation, and online auctions where vendors would have to bid online to obtain a master services agreement (MSA). So we had to be more flexible about what we charged.

Every salesperson wants to offer a discount—that's the nature of the beast—but we weren't in the business of doing jobs for little to no profit. My recommendation is to base discounts on whatever added value for your company, such as the aforementioned MSA. If your buyer wants a deal, you want a revenue commitment in return. For example, we continued to charge a premium for rush services because our turnaround time was something our competitors just couldn't match. When clients had to revisit our relationship if they were reassessing their vendors, they took into account our service/expertise/ability to be a one-stop shop.

Instead of restricting your salespeople on how much they could discount, I suggest you take a different approach. I recommend incentivizing your teams to increase gross margin on their sales. Be transparent on what you have to earn to cover your direct costs on each sale and empower your salespeople to set their own pricing. The higher they mark up a service, the more commission they'll make on the job and this will incentivize them to bring in the project with the highest margins. Plus, those who consistently sell with the highest margins should get enhancements on their commissions. When you're paid according to your margins, there's no place to hide. Those who consistently contract at lower margins should earn less and stand out for the wrong reasons.

I believe in tying the salespeople's and production's compensation to the company's revenue and profitability. With this practice, sales will work together with the production teams, rather than fight against them. In so many companies, the sales teams and production teams are out of alignment, with entirely different goals. My philosophy is that **if you want to get the whole organization on the same page, you must align everyone's incentives with the company's results.** I never wanted to lose a hard-won client because they were unhappy with something that happened during production. So not only do I recommend metrics and measurements for sales, but also the same for production. If you have a Platinum Club for sales, also have one for production; it's only fair.

My goal was to be the employer of choice. I recommend incentives like monthly wheelspins where the top performers earn additional prizes like trips, gift certificates, electronics, and spa days. If you create the culture of incentivizing everyone, you'll be a stronger, more profitable organization for it.

Share the Wealth

The language services and translation market is enormous—currently about $56 billion per year, so even though our company was incredibly successful, our market share wasn't huge.[9] And that was fine because I believe it's far more important to focus on client share. My strategy has always been to find ways to increase the individual client's business, because it's more cost-effective than courting entirely new clients. That is, as long as you don't have too much concentration in too few clients.

We taught sales teams to look for opportunities to provide our clients with more services, not only for the revenue, but because it heightened their dependence on us. For example, we translated many annual reports. We realized we could make our clients' jobs significantly easier if we not only translated the reports, but also helped them with the desktop publishing, printing, and binding. Instead of having to coordinate with multiple vendors, our clients knew they could give us their reports and we'd get the whole thing done.

We never wanted to take a job without also understanding its purpose. I refer you again to the annual reports; it wasn't enough for us just to translate the data and text. Translation was only half of the whole; the client would also need those bound hard copies for its shareholders. This is one of the reasons why we experienced such growth. We tried to understand our clients not by the jobs they gave us, but by **how our work product was a part of their larger ecosystem.** This paved the way for our being able to anticipate their needs, and that could entail anything from creating a virtual data room to providing consulting services. The more we expanded our services, the larger and more profitable we became.

Anticipating needs gave us the added benefit of diversifying our risk. We never wanted to have one of our clients be the bulk of our business, which is why we worked with every industry and language and pursued related lines of business. Again, this is why no one deal or client ever catapulted us into the stratosphere—what I'd call the Oprah effect. Instead, we literally got there one small project at a time.

When you can create exactly what your client needs without them even having to ask, price becomes an afterthought.

Reporting for Duty

Whether you're managing two or two thousand salespeople, the best tool to remain competitive is an end-of-day report. I've done these for myself ever since my first day of selling anything. I attribute these reports to helping scale our company. An EOD report is exactly what it sounds like—a report detailing all the actions you took during the day, because actions lead to sales. I very much managed by the numbers, first for myself, and then each person who reported to me until the company was so big that there were layers of management, and this is thanks to the use of EOD reports.

My EOD reports were a way to make myself accountable, knowing that the metrics mattered. Whether I was sending letters, making calls, or taking meetings, the numbers were important and I had to report them to myself each day. I'd also write down what key factors happened that day—how many bids or proposals I completed. I'd make note of new leads and prospects. This wasn't a formal process, and it's something I could accomplish with a five-minute freeform email to myself at the end of the day, back before there was CRM software.

Having this data at hand kept the important prospects at the top of my mind and aided me with my own planning process. In the very beginning, when everything was so amorphous, the EODs helped me structure my next steps and were a great way to remain organized. It bears repeating: actions lead to sales and I wanted to make sure I was tracking each action. If I knew that X number of letters led to Y projects and then Z multiple projects, why wouldn't I want to make sure I was creating that snowball effect? In my purview, every EOD was one step farther away from the dorm room.

EODs are something we rolled out to the whole company and our employees respected us for having them because they made running the entire business easier. I received EODs from my direct reports, although it was less about me going through their accomplishments and more about them being cognizant of what they'd done that day.

As an employer, you want a team who's itching to send you their reports—your superstars know exactly what they're doing right, and they are delighted to share this information with you. Any day of the year, I could ask our top performers how they were doing compared to their goals and they could immediately report their numbers off the cuff. A central theme in this chapter is the idea of not hiding. Sales isn't for those who want to sit in the back of the room and not raise their hands. Competition is not for the faint of heart.

You can't build a billion-dollar business out of wallflowers.

Third Prize Is You're Fired

Okay, I know I just said you can't build a billion-dollar company out of wallflowers, but I do believe that all things are possible in sales when you have a good coach. But if you don't have access to, say, legendary Duke University head coach and winningest college basketball coach of all time, Mike Krzyzewski—better known as Coach K—you're going to have a lot easier time getting your players to hit those layup shots if the teammates you draft aren't four feet tall.

When I was hiring salespeople, I looked for those with certain traits. I needed people who could deal with rejection because no matter how good they were, they were going to hear no. A lot. And that can be difficult without a thick skin. In my book, the ideal salesperson is ambitious, a self-starter. They thrive on competition, rather than avoid it. They don't wait around for someone to tell them what to do; they take the initiative. They're hungry for success, never complacent. But one more critical quality is something that's inherent, more of a personality trait rather than a skill.

I value a salesperson—or any person—who has natural curiosity. I had no idea how much until I recently attended a networking dinner with women who were at all stages of their careers. I was seated with two young attorneys, both starting out in the professional world. The ladies were kind and pleasant company to be seated with at a meal, but here's the rub. They didn't ask me a single question about myself. I found out all about them. We covered topics from the schools they attended, to their places of employment, to who they think makes the best bagel in the city (which is Tal Bagel, obviously). I got to know them because I was genuinely curious, but they couldn't say the same for me. When the dinner ended, they left, not having a clue as to who I was outside of the LIZ on my nametag and how I took my coffee at dessert. Ostensibly, given what I've done professionally and my propensity for spending copious amounts of money on legal fees, it seems like I might be. . .someone worth knowing? But these two lacked curiosity, and now we'll never know if there was any synergy between who and what I know and what they might need.

Curiosity is crucial, not just in sales but in life. It was such a contrast with all the amazing salespeople and employees I've worked with over the years. Our company grew like it did because we not only listened, but also kept our clients talking. Our competitive edge was coupling knowledge with service. Our sales team was able to delve into needs, having the temerity to ask that crucial question: "What else can we do for you?"

We were able to compete by dreaming big and winning, not only because we knew who our clients were, but because we knew who we were and we played to our strengths.

And you can, too.

Words of Wisdom

"The ability to learn faster from customers is the essential competitive advantage that startups must possess."

—Eric Ries

9

Investing

Turning a profit is only half the battle as you build your empire, even though it might feel as though you've finally reached the summit. However, if you're not reinvesting your profits wisely, all the effort you put into building your business will have been for naught.

In this chapter, we're going to examine the relationship between revenue growth and corporate spending to make sure you get the most bang out of every one of your hard-earned bucks, both professionally and personally.

Words of Wisdom

"We don't have to be smarter than the rest. We have to be more disciplined than the rest."

—Warren Buffett

Movin' on Up

I had a lot of big dreams in the early days of founding TransPerfect. I dreamed about seeing myself on stage (wearing something fabulous, possibly floral, probably pink), speaking to an audience full of employees, telling them, "This has been our most profitable year yet!" I dreamed about sitting across from marquee clients on foreign shores at an elegantly set table, our worlds and businesses coming together because of the power of translating shared meaning. I dreamed about having the means and wherewithal to go and do and buy whatever I wanted. But my biggest initial dream was not to have to make hundreds of daily cold calls from the same depressing room where I brushed my teeth and cooked my Ramen Pride noodles.

The first step to that stage and that dress and that dining table was getting out of the dorm room, if for no reason other than my state of mind. There was something disquieting about pitching a potential client on the quality of service I could offer while staring at a basket full of dirty laundry or muffling the sound of my cat horking up a hairball in the background. (Many of you discovered this yourselves during the early days of the pandemic.)

The natural inclination would have been to rent office space immediately, but I didn't want to spend money I didn't have. Much like I'd make myself earn that second cup of coffee or brisk walk around the block, I knew we had to have the revenue to cover a workspace outside of our living space.

Business school had drummed the lesson in my head that revenue is vanity and profit is sanity, so we weren't making the leap from the dorm until it was fiscally responsible. And the catch is **figuring out exactly *when* it's fiscally responsible to write that check to move up and out and when being too frugal creates diminishing returns.**

For all of those who take the leap before the financing appears, throwing themselves into the loving embrace of overwhelming debt, there's another faction who are too cautious, not scaling up when appropriate, staying too small by keeping costs too low. They don't bring on more staff, invest in greater marketing reach, or make capital improvements, so they can't compete for the bigger, more complicated projects, curtailing their ability to expand and diversify.

They refuse to spend money to make money.

If we were going to grow, we'd require the space and the personnel to do it, and the marketing to back it up, so we figured out how much we'd need to sell each month to cause that growth and made that our goal. I call this the *goldfish analogy*, as in a goldfish will never get larger than its tank allows. The growing fish will die without the right resources, like adequate food, room to swim, and clean, aerated water. So if you want bigger goldfish, it's necessary to put them in a tank that accommodates their growth and to clean up after them as they get bigger.

Thanks to the confidence vested in us by Cyprus Minerals, we were able to take the leap about six months into our tenure. We rented a shared executive suite for $625 a month, a sum that felt as exorbitant as it was necessary. If you're not familiar, an executive suite is a cluster of individual offices that share a central reception area, giving the impression of a larger company. Let me say this about an executive suite: it is far better than a dorm room for those clients dead set on visiting us.

As much as the suite represented a tangible achieved goal, the reality was anything but glamorous. This shared space boasted a tacky plastic sign out in front that I would rip down before a client visit, replacing it with a TransPerfect sign. Our foamboard sign wasn't exactly impressive either, especially because it was a mockup from the folks designing our logo. But when we stuck it to the door, it gave the impression that the whole office was ours and we knew perception was key. Unsexy reality time: if you tie every hire and each capital expenditure to a revenue goal, that's the surest way never to "get over your skis" financially.

We stayed in the $625-a-month office until we hit eight employees, and then we rented an extra office in that space for a total of $1,500 a month. By July of 1995, we'd outgrown the executive suite. The leap from $625 to $1,500 wasn't so huge, but to get to the next level, we'd have to spend considerably more. We always had the desire to run lean, but we couldn't let our desire to economize impact our ability to grow. In the mid-'90s, businesses didn't yet establish their presence and their bona fides on a fancy website. The way companies demonstrated they were contenders was in having an impressive address. If we wanted to prove to the marketplace we were a premier provider, we needed to have a premier address on our masthead, someplace iconic and impressive, like Park Avenue.

There was a landmark building at 3 Park Avenue that we just loved. Everything about it was right, from the impression of having a Park Avenue address to the endless amounts of space we could annex as we grew. Plus, the building was set on a diagonal, affording spectacular views of the city from every direction. It was our dream location, but it came at a price.

We took the leap.

For the (honestly terrifying) sum of $10,000 a month, the building not only gave us space for up to 20 densely packed employees and a real conference room, but they'd even take out our trash for us. We'd knew we'd have to sell at least $1,000,000 per year to pay for it, so that number became our sales goal, which we then doubled every year for the next few years.

Committing to that rent forced us to find a way to maintain our growth. This building was our New York home for over 20 years, and we were able to expand in it to more than 800 employees. We'd eventually take up five floors with an internal staircase connecting us all.

When we opened offices in other cities, the address was always important to us. For example, in our first satellite office in San Francisco, we found space in the iconic Embarcadero Center, because the address was not only impressive, but also home to the top-tier law firms we wanted as clients.

Back in the early days of the shared suite, one of my first salespeople used to say he couldn't wait for the day we were big enough to afford fresh flowers at the reception desk every week. Ironically, once we reached that point at 3 Park, I just couldn't do it. I bought silk ones instead, because I couldn't justify how spending so much on fresh flowers would help us continue to expand. Fresh flowers were vanity, not sanity.

We went from being a $1 million-a-year company to $5 million in 1997. There was no one factor that led to this leap; instead, it was a culmination of the slow, deliberate, steady growth, dictated by having hit our goals, thanks to staffing, sales, and marketing.

When we'd open an office in a new city, we did it with the utmost caution. We'd hire one person and put them in a shared space with a good address. That way we didn't have to worry about capital expenditures like office furniture. With every metric that one-person office hit, they were allowed to bring on another employee—again, only upon hitting metrics. Our approach was different than if we'd had investors, because a company is much more likely to be less frugal when they're not spending their own profits.

I can't stress enough that we never had a "unicorn event," the single big sale or acquisition that changed everything, along the scope of Facebook buying Instagram. Instead, our rise came from a mix of projects with Cyprus, JCPenney, and Debevoise & Plimpton, as well as diversifying product offerings and having more boots on the ground in new cities, **all implemented without taking on debt.** That year, Debevoise did make up about 50 percent of our business. I never wanted one client to control our destiny, so we took what we earned from them and kept investing in our growth to bring those percentages down as we broadened our reach through growing our sales teams and marketing outreach.

You don't need a unicorn event to become your own unicorn.

Liz's Life Lesson

Choose sanity over vanity.

There's No Such Thing as a Free Lunch

Even after the company had become the powerhouse organization I'd always dreamed about, my philosophy was to maintain tight reins on corporate spending. Plenty of tech giants were splashing out on outrageous perks for their employees, from Aeron chairs to frozen yogurt bars to massage therapists giving back rubs at the employee's desk. Some companies brought in Michelin chefs to cook for their people, and some invested in art collections that would rival that of a local museum.

No, we didn't do that.

Just the Facts

Seventy-five percent of venture-capital-backed companies never return cash to investors and in 30–40 percent of these cases, investors lose their entire initial investment.[1] And nine out of ten startups fail completely.

Because we didn't rely on any venture capital funding, we were always aware that the money we were spending was *ours* and I believed this factor kept us from becoming yet another statistic, especially as VCs often push companies to spend more money faster. Everyone wants to create a unicorn with a pearly horn and flowing rainbow mane, but sometimes what you need is a strong mule that can efficiently pull a plow.

Regardless of profitability, I couldn't bring myself to spend for the sake of spending. Hell, I even kept silk flowers in my own personal office. Granted, the office wasn't spartan; no one wants to be stuck somewhere that's dour and cheerless, reminiscent of the DMV. The workspace was very colorful, with pops of red, purple, and a gorgeous cobalt blue/multicolor globe mural based on our marketing material. (Eventually, HR asked me to change it to tranquil blue because they thought our colors were a little bit *too* exciting.) I remembered how impressed I was the first day I walked into Euramerica because it was wide open and modern, and every desk had a brand-new Macintosh computer. I felt like I was glimpsing the future, and I wanted to re-create that feeling for my employees, a vibe that was a huge draw for other startups at the time.

Even though there was pressure to keep up with the dot-com culture, I never did see how having a foosball table would increase our profitability, like everyone else had at the turn of the millennium. However, many years into our tenure, we did set up a lounge with couches and a Ping-Pong table on the production floor, because the production team was always stuck in the office. They were the troopers handling the deluge of business, so we wanted to make sure they had an outlet. (But to be clear, Ping-Pong was not for closers. Sales sat in densely packed cubicles on another floor.)

For a while, in order to motivate our people, we offered benefits like Free Lunch Friday. We'd do birthday celebrations and would offer complimentary juice and soda, but as we progressed, we couldn't believe how much the perks cut into our profit margin. Here's the thing: When you have an underperforming employee who comes to the office and gets rewarded with a cushy work atmosphere full of free food without having put in the effort, it doesn't motivate them to reach their goals. I learned that when these perks were expected, they lost their luster and people didn't appreciate them. We chose to stop the superfluous perks, instead channeling that money into what would produce results. Those free lunches benefited no one, as we'd eventually learn during exit interviews. Plus, I didn't want to hire salespeople who were excited about the idea of a gratis burrito; I wanted people who'd maximize their profit margin so they could buy themselves a gourmet lunch at Balthazar.

Instead of turning your office into an all-you-can-eat buffet, I suggest you use those profits to incentivize your people, giving them the opportunity to earn more than anyone else in the industry.

We found perks to be far more effective when they were based on performance, so we motivated our people not with frozen yogurt, but with Platinum Clubs and wheelspins.

Ours was a true meritocracy.

We took what we didn't spend on little treats and funneled that cash into training programs, too. We believed that when we had the best-trained personnel in the industry, they'd be more invested in and indebted to the company, and that was the greatest value we could add.

A Snowball's Chance

We grew because we invested a healthy chunk of our profits in ramping up our sales team. The more salespeople we had on the team, the more volume we could create and the more repeat business we could generate.

My goal was to make our sales organization the largest, most talented, and most highly compensated in the industry. I can't stress this enough because I've known so many entrepreneurs with wonderful services or products who neglect to make this a top priority. It's one of the biggest reasons small businesses fail or never become big businesses.

One of the most valuable things we did in the beginning was to include a printed Rolodex card in our mailers. Rolodexes were a round, rotating, alphabetized card filing device that everyone used to maintain their business contacts' phone numbers and addresses before the digital age. (If they're before your time, ask your parents.) They were so important back then that even now, people use the term "Rolodex" to refer to a central cache of information. In those days, when you'd get a new business card, you'd either staple it to a blank card or transfer the info to a blank Rolodex card. That we sent them out preprinted and ready to insert was revolutionary at the time. This made it easy for clients to contact us. I imagine the contemporary version of this would be to airdrop a LinkedIn profile, but everyone can do that, so there's no real apples-to-apples comparison.

We felt the snowball effect as we added staff. More people meant more calls and letters, which led to more projects, which led to more profits, which led to more staffing which led to...well, you get the idea.

Words of Wisdom

"To grow rapidly, you need to make something you can sell to a big market. That's the difference between Google and a barbershop. A barbershop doesn't scale."

—Paul Graham

Fighting for Crumbs

If you want to create a company with longevity, understand that your product offerings must change and expand with the times. You must be nimble. We remained competitive because we perpetually invested in introducing new products and services to accommodate client requests and needs, such as litigation support, staffing services, and multiple technologies. Air hockey tables just can't deliver that same ROI.

Assuming the marketplace will remain the same is the kiss of death for most businesses. For example, in 2010, Crumbs Bake Shop was on the fast track to stratospheric success, as one of the names on Inc.'s 500 Fastest-Growing Companies list.[2] They were riding high on the buttercream wave of the cupcake trend, which was beginning to peak at the beginning of the 2010s, thanks in part to television shows like *Cake Boss*, *Cupcake Wars*, and *DC Cupcakes*. Cupcakes in that decade were as ubiquitous as Pet Rocks in the 1970s and parachute pants in the 1980s. Crumbs doubled down on their business model, rapidly expanding and opening stores across the country.

The issue was that cupcakes were a fad, like rocks as pets and pants made from trash bags, and not a mainstay, like coffee and lunch. Most people didn't buy cupcakes daily, especially because Crumbs' cupcakes were too large to be anything but a special occasion treat as consumers started to become more fat- and carb-conscious. Take their vanilla cupcake, for example. Crumbs' offerings were 780 calorie monsters, as opposed to the cute, compact 250 calorie cupcakes sold at competitors such as Georgetown Bakery.[3] Eventually they did offer smaller cakes, but that's it. Because Crumbs didn't serve options like soups, salads, or sandwiches, there was no reason for hungry shoppers to stop in, save for that special-occasion purchase or a desire to get Type II diabetes. And as their competition in the cupcake market increased, instead of diversifying, they put all their eggs into the expansion basket, literally. They invested, but they didn't innovate, which is why they went from a $13 share price to 15 cents and all 48 of their stores closed.

I'm not saying green juice could have saved them, but I'm also not saying it couldn't have.[4]

Ironically, the brand Rolodex is still around, and the company sells a variety of desk organization tools, yet I can't imagine how much more successful they could have been if they'd built on their brand and transitioned to providing CRM software.

Diamonds on the Soles of Her Shoes

Years into the process, my dream of being able to go and do and buy whatever I wanted came true. I knew the only way to hold onto it was to properly invest what I'd earned.

Also, the truth is, I don't find personal investing itself particularly interesting. I do not wake up early every Saturday morning and rush to log onto Barrons.com, breathlessly awaiting Jack Hough's latest editorial. I don't keep a television tuned to CNBC all day, and I can't imagine owning a Bloomberg terminal. Yes, I made investments myself in the beginning, but equities aren't my passion. The bulk of my strategy was less about the stock market and more about not buying what I couldn't afford and increasing my income and savings each year. As soon as I could, I turned my earnings over to professionals because thinking about how to grow my own money gave me no pleasure.

We took very little out of the company, because we were so focused on reinvesting in the company, as that's the surest way to make it grow. Reinvestment is key. However, there's also an argument to be made for not putting everything back into the company. Danny Briere offered this perspective when it comes to taking money out, telling me:

> My first big mistake was continuing to invest in my company to grow, grow, grow, and never take a chunk out for myself. I was young and had no real mentors to advise me otherwise. When the telecom crash came, two weeks shy of closing my eight-digit sale of the company, it all crashed, overnight, and I lost it all. Taking care of yourself and making sure you can always walk away with something is really important. Remember, you can overinvest to the detriment of your future. You never know when the world will collapse in a second and if everything is tied up in your company, it could truly have been all for naught.

Regardless of what you do with your profits, I'd be remiss if I didn't recognize how far women have come regarding the opportunity of whether we choose to manage our money ourselves. In my own lifetime, a woman wasn't allowed to open a line of credit on her own, even if she earned more than her spouse. (Think for a moment exactly how outrageous that sounds today.) Regardless of her circumstances, a woman would have to have a cosigner. This didn't change until the Fair Credit Opportunity Act of 1974 made it illegal for financial institutions to discriminate against applicants for any reason, including race, national origin, religion, or gender.[5]

Maybe that's why women are often so reticent to discuss money. In a survey, Merrill Lynch found that 61 percent of women would rather discuss their own deaths than talk about money![6] This is particularly problematic because 90 percent of women will be solely responsible for their own finances in their lifetime, whether it's due to death, divorce, or the decision to stay single.[7] Speaking to those readers who are women, we can't truly take control of our financial livelihoods if the subject remains taboo, so I encourage you to talk about money (even if it makes you uncomfortable or bores you to tears).

When I finally had some money, I chose to let the professionals invest it wisely, instead of splurging on every single luxury I'd forgone while building the company. I loved shoes, purses, and dresses, but I loved the feeling of security more. (That's not to say I don't treat myself, of course.) I knew I needed to be able to take care of myself financially and never be dependent on anyone else, so I bought my first apartment in 1997 for $386,000 and I had to overbid to get it. The building was brand new and modern, and only a 10-minute walk from the office. I was the first person ever to live in my one-bedroom apartment. The best part was the building's name—The Future. How could I not want to buy a place with that name? I lived there for three years and sold it for $595,000. I invested in The Future, indeed.

In addition to buying that piece of real estate, I invested in enriching myself, meaning I never stopped trying to grow and learn. I read every business book I could get my hands on. I kept current on business news by daily reads of *Crain's*, the *New York Times*, and the *Wall Street Journal*, often picking up the *Financial Times* and the *Economist*, too. (That doesn't mean I didn't read the occasional *Cosmo* or *People* as well. Who among us wasn't invested in whether Bennifer would ever get back together?) I learned from my peers at YEO and YPO and attended lectures and conferences whenever possible. There's a misconception that once you make it, you're done, but that's the surest way to stagnate. Learning is a lifetime commitment, and I read just as voraciously today.

Much like I never had the Facebook-acquisition-style sale at the company, I didn't wake up one day with the lightning bolt of realization that I'd worked myself into more wealth than I could ever spend. I didn't suddenly buy an island, a plane, or a boat large enough to park next to Leo DiCaprio's in Cannes. I don't even own a Birkin bag, much to my friends' dismay. What I did realize is that my earnings afforded me the privilege to learn more and to give more, and that's when I became serious about charitable work (which I'll discuss in Chapter 15).

Perhaps you'd think that not having to worry about the price of gas or the cost of tuition brings a certain kind of freedom, and to an extent it does. The difficulties come in being a parent of means. Are my children's vacations better than most? Probably. However, the offspring of wealthy parents have 20–30 percent higher levels of anxiety than the less affluent, and those children are more likely to struggle with drug and alcohol usage, so it's a double-edged sword.[8]

I've had to make sure not to be indulgent with my sons, because they will be happiest growing up understanding how to solve their own problems, like my family taught me. The best way to ensure their future success is for them to develop their own work ethic and find their own way. That's why they got the same kinds of minimum-wage jobs over school breaks that every other typical teenager in America has. I'm so proud to watch them developing their own understanding of hard work and accountability. The most loving act their father and I have done for them is not to swoop in and solve their problems by writing a check. If we did, we'd have denied them the opportunity to experience the satisfaction of overcoming obstacles and working for their own success. . .even though the mom in me wants to stomp down every barrier for them.

So I guess I could say that my dreams have changed since the early days. Investing enough in myself and my company was crucial to getting to wear that dress on that stage and at that dinner. But now my plans are to invest in something larger than just a language solutions company.

My goal is to invest in a better future for everyone.

Words of Wisdom

"If a man is proud of his wealth, he should not be praised until it is known how he employs it."

—Socrates

Refining the Purpose

10

Communicating

Honest, open, productive communication is a key ingredient to creating and maintaining any relationship you want to thrive, be it businesses or personal. That two-way dialogue between parties, whether it's a husband and wife, a family or a friend group, a manager and employee, or a company and its customer base, is crucial to maintain equilibrium, establish expectations, and pivot appropriately when problems arise.

Think of effective communication as the gluten in a loaf of bread—it's the magical, miraculous ingredient that makes everything come together and change for the better.[1]

So let's have a conversation about the art of having a conversation.

Words of Wisdom

"The most important thing in communication is to hear what isn't being said."

—Peter Drucker

(Brand) Killing Communication

In 1982, seven Chicago-area residents died after taking potassium cyanide–laced capsules of Extra-Strength Tylenol. The pills had been tampered with after production, and the tainted product was placed back on grocery and drug store shelves, where they were purchased and ingested by the victims. As horrific as this sounds, the worst part is that the crime is still unsolved, and no one has ever been charged with these murders. The only upside to this case—other than it being fodder for true crime podcasts—is that the event wasn't a brand-killer for Tylenol. Tylenol exists as a trusted product today thanks to the way Johnson & Johnson communicated with the public about the tragedy.

As soon as McNeil Consumer Products, a J&J subsidiary, discovered that their product had been tainted, they leapt into action, immediately recalling more than 31 million bottles, instead of dragging their heels with an investigation or limiting the recall to a geographic area. The company stopped advertising the product and worked tirelessly to alert consumers to the potential dangers, regardless of what blanketing the media meant for their own bottom line. The national nightly news featured the deaths at the top of the hour for six weeks; the story was impossible to ignore and the product's fate seemed sealed.

Within weeks, J&J's share of the over-the-counter consumer market dropped from 35 percent to 8 percent.[2] Per Judith Rehak in an article for the *New York Times*, "Marketers predicted that the Tylenol brand, which accounted for 17 percent of the company's net income in 1981, would never recover from the sabotage."[3] Yet despite the experts' prevailing wisdom, Tylenol successfully returned to the marketplace two months later.

What made the difference? How did they win back the seemingly irretrievable consumers' trust? How did they protect buyers and redeem their brand when no one thought it was possible?

Through clear, concise, candid communication, of course.

The crisis communication employed by Chairman James Burke and his seven-member strategy team is a case study in best practices, as the company's priority was to inform and protect every consumer and worry about reputation management only in the aftermath.

Let's break down how they did it.

First, the company took full responsibility for the incident, apologizing and accepting all the blame. Their communication was transparent and ongoing, so the public was informed. Then they took it a step further by not only recalling and refunding purchases but creating new tamper-proof packaging to prevent anything similar from ever happening again, spending $100 million in the process. (Their move forced their competitors to do the same, as well.) Within a year, J&J's stock price would bounce back and they'd regain most of their lost market share, and Burke would go on to eventually win the Presidential Medal of Freedom.

Compare this example to the blow taken to the formerly pristine reputation of the Toyota Motor Corporation over crash data on its Camry model. In 2002, the company sent a bulletin to US dealerships about an electrical issue, explaining that due to a problem with the throttle, cars were unexpectedly accelerating. Later, Toyota changed their story and claimed these sudden bursts of speed were due to an issue with the floormats. They denied evidence of the service bulletin, ostensibly because ignoring the issue or replacing a rug was more cost-effective than repairing millions of computer sensors.

Instead of an immediate recall or any degree of transparency, the company allowed the issue to fester, also attributing these crashes to user error. *They literally blamed the victims*. But it wasn't until consumers began connecting the dots on social media that the whole cover-up exploded in a (preventable) PR nightmare for the company.

When Jim Lentz, the president and CEO of Toyota Motor Sales in the US, went on the *Today* show, such was his subterfuge and poor communication during Matt Lauer's questioning that 56 percent of those surveyed after seeing the interview said they wouldn't buy a Toyota, up from the 37 percent from before he spoke.[4]

I have to wonder where Olivia Pope from *Scandal* was during all of this.

Toyota refused to be transparent, even when testifying in front of Congress. The CEO from the Japanese parent company was highly criticized for his evasive answers. Ultimately, the company was sanctioned, sales declined, and the company lost $2.47 billion (and an additional $1.1 billion in a class action lawsuit) and 15 percent of its stock's value. The most devastating blow was the loss of consumer confidence because they chose not to communicate honestly with their previously loyal customer base, opening the door for startup brands like Kia and Hyundai to become contenders.[5]

Tacos, *Sí o No?*

Both the J&J and Toyota examples are on the extreme side; life and death may not often be on the line for your clients. But if your company isn't leveling with your buyers, you could kill your business.

As an example of what I mean, let's say you're trying to fly from Chicago to New York on whatever airline gave you the best deal. You arrive at the airport in plenty of time and you're just starting to line up at the gate when the gate agent announces a delay. There are two ways that airline can play this, and as a road warrior I can tell you I've experienced both plenty of times. While each is about as desirable as a middle seat, one approach is far superior.

In terms of customer satisfaction and repeat business, it's far more effective to explain to passengers that there will be an hour-long delay because of X and that it is being fixed by Y. If passengers know they have an hour, they'll still be aggravated, but at least this way, they'll have time to grab a quick (and surprisingly great) lunch at Tortas Frontera by Rick Bayless or make that phone call or shop for souvenir sweatshirts that say CHICAGO on them. Again, it's not ideal to be delayed, but the margaritas will take the edge off.

Yet so often, and with full knowledge that it takes 60 minutes to solve the problem, airlines will instead push back the boarding time in 10-minute increments because of their own internal metrics, leading to unhappy and occasionally aggressive passengers who worry they'll lose their place crowding the gate if they even leave to use the restroom. Passengers are going to be far more forgiving—and less prone to rage tweeting—when they have all the information and their expectations are managed, especially if the delay permits them to partake in delicious tacos and churros con chocolate. Informing your clients of what's happening, especially during a crisis, is never a bad call. In the airline's case, passengers will be less likely to choose a different carrier for their next flight.

Words of Wisdom

"Honesty is always the best policy, even when it's not the trend."

—Steve Covey

Survey Says

I am a huge proponent of open communication. In pursuit of this goal, I implemented many different ways of gauging client satisfaction to make sure there was a flow of information. In the early days, before there were layers of management between me and our clients, I made frequent calls and often had in-person meetings with everyone on our roster. Whatever we were doing right or wrong, I wanted to know.

Once we were bigger and I didn't have the opportunity for one-on-one time with everyone, our 600-person sales team kept the conversations going, because relationship management was an important part of their jobs. The sales team made sure the clients understood not only what we were doing but why. Much like I discussed understanding the whole ecosystem of a client project in the last chapter, we wanted to communicate with our clients how they fit into our company's ecosystem. Fortunately, I was able to get direct feedback at VIP events, such as cooking classes and trips to Miraval, as well as at the educational, content-based programming we put on at places like the Mandarin Oriental.

As we grew, we implemented ways to stay in touch with our clients, such as sending those bottomless containers of chocolates. We'd reach out with cards and gifts for those industries that could accept them, and experiences for clients in regulated industries like pharmaceuticals that couldn't. In every way we could, we communicated how important they were to us.

We supplemented our efforts to keep communication flowing with a couple of different survey tools to make sure everyone was happy. We'd send an annual survey, which was valuable because these questions illuminated longer-term issues we might have been having.

Although, let's be honest, most clients weren't reticent in telling us what we were doing wrong. At all.

More immediately, we'd follow up with the client for feedback after every single job because if we didn't meet expectations, we needed to know at once. As Toyota learned too late, we never wanted problems to smolder because that makes them exponentially more difficult to resolve, like in a restaurant where a good server will return to check on the diner's status so they can fix any errors after the first bite, and not after the entire meal. The faster our team uncovered a problem or opportunity, the more quickly we could address the issue or implement the suggestion. Many of our best products and services came directly from the surveys we collected, so this feedback was invaluable.

The key to surveying is to act on the information attained; it's not enough to just collect it. When surveys highlight a problem, I believe in employing a rapid resolution protocol. Step one is to get together with the client either in person or on the phone and apologize profusely. There's a competing school of thought about never admitting guilt, particularly when there are reputations and millions of dollars at stake. Per Kathryn Phillips, an ethics professor at Columbia, CEOs and corporations don't like to admit guilt, not just because this could open the door to crushing liabilities from plaintiffs' counsel but also because it's embarrassing. She says, "One of the basic kinds of psychological needs of human beings is to save face—right?—and to not look stupid, and not look like they don't know what they're doing. And people who are in powerful positions, and in charge, oftentimes feel that pressure even more so."[6]

My philosophy is, how can anyone learn from a mistake if they don't first take ownership of it? Specifically, most of our issues had to do with the translations themselves—which meant that the errors could be either subjective or objective. Meaning can be amorphous in translation. Regardless of interpretation, we would apologize to the client that they didn't receive what they wanted.

Admitting fault isn't a sign of weakness; rather, it shows the company has the strength and integrity to own an error and sets a positive example for all employees.

Just the Facts

Per a Gallup poll, two of the top five qualities of a great manager are creating a culture of accountability and fostering open communication and trust.[7]

After the admission and apology, the next step is to work out a plan of action with the client to make sure this problem never happens again. For us, this often led to new procedures in the production process, which not only prevented the issue from happening with one client but would positively impact all of them.

Many times, an issue would be resolved before it was brought to me, because we empowered our employees at every level to take ownership of problems, following the admission/apology/plan path. We made sure our processes weren't so onerous that most problems couldn't be resolved quickly and without escalation.

When a client is unhappy, minutes count.

Do I Need to Turn This Office Around?

Communication within the company is just as important as having open lines with the client. My approach is best described as initiative-taking, because it's always better to address issues as soon as they arise. For example, say an employee showed up a couple of minutes late for their shift. The first time, perhaps it's an anomaly; maybe track work on their subway line delayed their commute or there was an accident on the expressway. It happens and it's not a problem. However, assuming the employee doesn't apologize and it's not an anomaly, our expectation was for their manager to have a conversation about this tardiness immediately. Otherwise, it would set the precedent that it was okay to show up a few minutes late when the subway wasn't delayed, leading to bad longer-term habits. Unacceptable behavior should always be discussed the moment it occurs so it can be nipped in the bud.

Liz's Life Lesson
Ignoring it until it goes away is never a strategy.

Conflicts between employees are always going to arise, especially in a high-stress environment, no matter how professional and diligent your team is. It's human nature, and misunderstandings happen. The company's sales team was comprised entirely of alphas, so heads could often butt over client ownership and percentages. Or sometimes production wouldn't feel respected by the sales team; perhaps sales spoke rudely to them in an email. Regardless of the circumstances, when two of my employees would clash, I would put them both in a room together with me (or another member of management) and we would discuss the problem as a group. They'd each tell me their side of the story, and together we'd unpack the problem. When you have everyone face-to-face, it's harder to let someone get away with a lie (unless you're George Santos, apparently) and people tend to be nicer to each other and more willing to extend grace, so head-on was the most expedient way to find a resolution.

FYI, I feel like this could work for the rest of Congress, too.

Communication Includes a U

Sometimes leaders have to communicate in a way that scares them. There may be times they must, say, deliver bad news to Wall Street or disappoint a loyal client due to circumstances beyond their control. It can be tough. And while the situation may actually be benign, nonetheless the very act of communication makes them anxious.

For example, years back, in 2007, we brought in former Secretary of State Colin Powell as our keynote speaker to discuss leadership. This was for our company's 15-year anniversary and it was the last time we brought our entire team from around the world to NYC. At the time, we were about 750 employees. As you can imagine, Powell gave an incredibly inspiring speech and had the crowd in the palm of his hand. Later that night we held our company party, as we always did around the holidays, this time at Chelsea Piers.

I remember that night like it was yesterday, because I felt extraordinarily nervous about addressing that huge group. Not only did I need to get up to speak in front of what would be the largest gathering of my career, but my speech was on the heels of them having listened to Secretary Powell, who was such a powerful orator.

The easiest and most comfortable thing would have been to skip giving that motivational speech. But that wasn't exactly an option. So I composed myself, took a deep breath, smiled, and did it anyway.

Words of Wisdom

"I get nervous when I don't get nervous. If I'm nervous I know I'm going to have a good show."

—Beyoncé

What I learned that night at Chelsea Piers is that no matter how many times I've spoken in public, I will always have butterflies, but that fear can't be a reason not to push forward. And of course, the big lesson here is that it's okay (and actually more common than not) to feel afraid, as long as you acknowledge it, channel it to build adrenaline, and do it anyway. The feeling of success after each speech makes the challenge all the more worth it.

Words of Wisdom

"If you have stage fright, it never goes away. But then I wonder: is the key to that magical performance because of the fear?"

—Stevie Nicks

Agree to Disagree

A leader should foster an environment where employees are free to disagree with management. The last thing any company needs is a bunch of yes-people. For example, Unilever's Dove division found this out when they posted an advertisement that was universally panned for displaying a racist trope. The GIF was a series of three women removing their shirts, revealing consistently lighter-skinned women in each frame after using Dove body wash. It doesn't matter that Dove was (ham-handedly) attempting to celebrate bodily diversity; what mattered is the impression the ad left on the consumer and *it was not positive*. (I can't help but think this wouldn't have happened when my dad was on their ad team.)

On Facebook, user Abby Macklin wrote, "I mean anyone with eyes can see how offensive this is. Not one person on your staff objected to this?"[8] The ad had to pass through layers of review, so my assumption is that no one felt empowered enough to save the company from making a terrible error in judgment. Perhaps everyone on the management team was white and, as a result, were seeing this only through their white lens. (We'll get more into the need for diversity in the boardroom in Chapter 13.)

When you foster an environment where your employees are free to disagree, you spark conversations that generate ideas. We took our first 20 or so employees to a resort in the Bahamas as a reward for completing a grueling multi-week project, with many all-nighters. During a meeting at the resort, we had so many rapid-fire ideas and disagreements flying around that we had to institute a policy that whoever was holding the camera was the person permitted to speak.

Did it get loud? Was there yelling? Yes.

Did we spark conversations and generate ideas? Absolutely. **Sometimes it gets loud, and that is okay**. (Did the margaritas help? Oh, God, yes.)

Bullies can exist in any organization, no matter how well run, so it's imperative for the leader not to let the loudest always have the last word. Leaders should make sure they don't allow themselves to be bullies either. Their job is to treat employees with respect and to serve them, never lording their power over their people. People can fear retaliation, so as a leader, you should take employees aside and speak with them offline, because getting perspective from the quiet is as important as hearing it from the loud.

Who's Up for a Game of One-on-One?

If you want to hear every voice in your company, you have to make sure you're speaking with them frequently. Ever since we were a handful of people, I've been a huge proponent of weekly one-on-one meetings, meaning managers with their respective employees. They're crucial because they facilitate communication in both directions. They're an excellent time to touch base not only about day-to-day issues and performance, but also for long-term planning. If you're not soliciting your employees' feedback, you will eventually lose them. Fact.

I learned this lesson the hard way in the early days when one of my staff members quit unexpectedly. We worked side by side day in and day out (literally), but unfortunately, I wasn't doing proper one-on-ones. If I had, I would have known there was a problem. My staff member's issues with me/the company/their role/their potential for advancement would have been clear, and I would have tried to resolve them, but I couldn't and we lost a talented person.

This experience reinforced to me the importance of one-on-ones and taught me that as we grew, we needed to institute skip-level meetings so that our employees knew they were welcome to speak with their boss's boss. These are also crucial because it can be difficult for an employee to open up about issues with the manager when speaking to that manager. When not allowed the opportunity to skip a level, the employee is more likely to say everything is fine.

A word? Fine is *not fine*.

Fine is a deceptively bad term because it's not definitive. Fine is what we say when we'd rather say something else but aren't comfortable or it's not worth it to do so. It's like when the server asks you how your lunch is and your salad is full of the fennel you'd requested they leave off. You're not allergic and you can just pick off the fronds and you're pressed for time, so it's not a terrible imposition. Still, you're aggravated that the server either didn't listen to you or didn't spot-check the chef's work before handing you the plate. So maybe instead of connecting with your lunch companion and being present, you're in your head, thinking, "Licorice is the devil's candy."

While your lunch was *fine*, meaning technically acceptable, it actually wasn't because that stupid fennel threw you off your purpose, which was to be present for your lunch companion. Your real, not-fine opinion will be reflected in the tip and your reticence to return to that establishment. *Fine* doesn't help anyone grow or improve. I'd much prefer an employee have a higher-level outlet who's empowered to help them, rather than leaving them to their own devices, which may include bad-mouthing their boss to their coworkers and bringing down morale.

That's why in addition to client surveys, I advocate using employee surveys because if you can't measure it, you can't manage it. The conundrum is whether the surveys should be anonymous or attributed. If people sign their names, you might not get the whole story. But if people don't sign their names, then you'll find out more details, but won't know who the issue is coming from and you probably can't resolve it. I wanted to act and resolve problems, making ours the most desirable workplace. I never wanted to have a case of people telling us, "I love my boss but can't stand senior management," because what they were really saying was, "I don't like the company." I believe that a mix of anonymous and attributed surveys are the most effective.

My goal was to create a culture of equality where every single person, regardless of position or tenure, could look the CEO in the eye and say, "Good morning!" and would expect the same from the CEO. The best bosses serve their employees, trying to create satisfied workers and amazing careers, because their happiness translates to the clients and to revenue and profit, and one-on-ones are a critical way to get there.

No, This Could *Not* Have Been an Email

Harsh truth: we rely too much on email and it's become a communication shortcut that I despise. Email takes away a degree of understanding and so often leads to a misconstrued message because tone is subjective. My strong preference is a face-to-face conversation, delivered with kindness and respect. When possible, it's always more effective to convey your message in person. (Do not even start me on the comedy of errors that results from texting. The last thing any leader needs is an inner-office battle royale because Paula in Payroll misinterpreted Accounting Adam's thumbs-up emoji. She sits three seats away! Walk over there and tell her, "Yes," for crying out loud.) Given a choice, I always default to in-person conversation, with the phone or a Zoom call if that's not possible. It's just too hard to convey tone otherwise.

I'm not the only one who feels this way about email. Researchers at the University of California, Irvine, studied the effects of email on a recipient's physical stress levels by measuring heart-rate variability. They learned that the longer a person spent on an email in a given hour, the longer they felt levels of stress.[9] This is why countries like France have created labor laws that limit the requirement for employees to be connected via email in after-work hours. *C'est si bon*.

Just the Facts

Workers spend an average of 30 hours per week checking their email.[10] (Note: the 30 hours do not include hours spent reading and answering those emails. So when do they have time to do their actual job?)

If you must use email—and of course you do and you will—my rule is, "Never write anything you wouldn't want to see printed on the front page of the *New York Times*" (or whatever your favorite paper is) because you never know how that email might be used. We learned this the hard way. One of our top salespeople once bad-mouthed via email a client who had given us a $1 million project. Those careless words got back to the client and ended up costing us about $500,000 in discounts in order to make amends. That one hurt. I know it can be hard to take the high road, but if you just can't, at least don't leave the kind of paper trail that will knock six figures off the bottom line.

And Then We Came to the End

Regardless of the careers you offer and how free-flowing your communication may be, there will come a time when you lose people.

It's part of the business lifecycle. I found it important to understand exactly why people were leaving, so we always conducted exit interviews. It's so useful to get the unvarnished opinion, even though I'd have preferred to learn about bad bosses or inappropriate behavior before employees decided to leave.

I read every single exit interview that my company ever conducted because that's how valuable I found them. These exit interviews helped uncover a host of problem areas that we were then able to address, such as employees who showed up at their new jobs and had to wait a week for a desk or a computer. I learned the importance of our first impression and how that impacted our new hire's happiness, so instead of having parties when people quit, I recommend celebrating on people's first day instead. The interviews showed us areas where we could improve, even down to tiny issues like "Why does the 40th floor have an espresso machine and the 39th doesn't?"

Think about it—if a coffee maker is the one thing standing between your star employee and their happiness at your company, wouldn't you want to know?

Just the Facts

In a survey of 400 companies with 100,000 employees each, reporter David Grossman cited an average loss per company of $62.4 million per year due to poor communication to and between employees.[11]

Honest, productive communication is necessary, not just for companies, but for anyone in any kind of a relationship. Communication is how we connect what we do with why we do it, like when JFK greeted a janitor at NASA who was mopping after hours. Kennedy said, "Hi, I'm Jack Kennedy. Why are you working so late?" Given the culture of NASA, and what had been communicated to him, the janitor understood the importance of his role. The janitor replied, "Well,

Mr. President, I'm helping put a man on the moon."[12] Communication is our reason for being.

So, consider how you can break some bread and start some conversations today.

Words of Wisdom

"If you want to build a ship, don't drum people together to collect wood and don't assign them the tasks and work, but rather teach them to long for the endless immensity of the sea."

—Antoine de Saint-Exupéry

11

Leading

A common misconception is that to be a leader, you have to be the boss; this is simply untrue. While the terms are used interchangeably (admittedly by me as well), they aren't the same thing because they entail different qualities. Not all leaders are bosses, and not all bosses are leaders. If mentioning this difference doesn't spark an immediate flash of recognition about some of your former managers, you've been lucky.

According to Leon Ho, the founder and CEO of Lifehack, the difference between a boss and a leader is, "A boss's main priority is to efficiently cross items off of the corporate to-do list, while a true leader both completes tasks and works to empower and motivate the people he or she interacts with on a daily basis. A leader is someone who works to improve things instead of focusing on the negatives. People acknowledge the authority of a boss, but people cherish a true leader."[1] Are you nodding your head yet? If not, think of it like this—the Michael Scott character on *The Office* is a boss; Ron Swanson on *Parks and Recreation* is a leader.

In this chapter, we'll break down what it means to *lead* others via my Five Ps of Leadership, and not just boss them around. But remember—none of the Five Ps will matter if you're not coming from a foundation of integrity first.

I recently wrote about the concept of integrity for *Forbes*, saying, "There is such a thing as the common good, and integrity is at its core our willingness to both understand that and put it into action. It involves the recognition of community and our responsibility to avoid harming others either maliciously *or* through neglect. It demands good intent in thought and action deriving from a respect for the basic dignity of those around you. All of these are things which have, of late, been in short supply amongst our gilded class leadership, and all of these are things we need to reclaim."[2]

To quote William McRaven in *The Wisdom of the Bullfrog*, "There are always examples of successful people who lack scruples, who have no moral compass yet have made billions of dollars and driven their industries to new heights. But more often than not, that lack of integrity, doing wrong instead of right, can manifest itself in a toxic work culture, a failed business, or a personal tragedy…. Doing what is right matters because, when exhibited by a leader on a daily basis, it develops the culture of the institution, and it develops the next generation of leaders."

True leaders exemplify integrity, and are not dishonest or bullies, and do not discriminate or harass. When they see this behavior in others, whether fellow leaders, their employees, or even their bosses, they do not tolerate it and they speak up to eliminate it. They risk whatever repercussions there may be, including even losing their jobs, in order to do what's right.

Please do keep this concept front of mind as we explore the Five Ps.

Words of Wisdom

"The supreme quality for leadership is unquestionable integrity. Without it, no real success is possible, no matter whether it is on a section gang, a football field, in an army, or in an office."

—Dwight D. Eisenhower

Truly, Madly, Deeply

Every leader's style is unique. Imagine how different the experience would have been working for Jack Welch versus Jim Henson. Henson, creator of the Muppets, was a gentle visionary. He was known for his huge heart and beloved for his sense of humor and creativity. In an article for *Fast Company*, Muppets writer Jerry Juhl talked about Henson's spirit. "One of the images that I think we all have of Jim that we've seen repeatedly is Jim standing in the studio with his hand in the air and a puppet and he's laughing uncontrollably. Everything has come to a complete stop, and that kind of infectious enthusiasm kind of spread through all casts and crews, and Jim balanced that with a desire to do the work as well as possible. So, you were working at the top of your form, but you were also having as much fun as possible, and I think that was very infectious."[3] One assumes that Jack Welch, the clean-shaven, straitlaced former chair of General Electric, would have simply slapped the puppets out of all the kindly hippies' hands.

However, that perception might not be entirely true.

In fact, Welch wrote in an early 1990s annual report to shareholders, "We want GE to become a company where people come to work every day in a rush to try something they woke up thinking about the night before. We want them to go home from work wanting to talk about what they did that day, rather than trying to forget about it. We want factories where the whistle blows and everyone wonders where the time went, and someone suddenly wonders aloud why we need a whistle. We want a company where people find a better way, every day, of doing things; and whereby shaping their own work experience, they make their lives better and your company best."[4]

What did these two incredibly divergent yet still effective leaders have in common?

The first of my Five Ps of Leadership—*passion*.

It's crucial that a leader is passionate about what they do. Regardless of our work ethic, education, and experience, our company never would have gotten off the ground if we weren't passionate about the notion of helping the world connect through translation. Without passion, we could never even have dreamed about all the hours we'd spend in the office. With every project we sold, no matter how small, we saw the purpose and value of our efforts. We enhanced other companies' and people's ability to communicate internationally, which allowed them to grow and diversify, saving everything from jobs to lives. To be clear, **I was able to work an obscene number of hours in the early days because it never felt like I was working; I was doing my own version of the NASA janitor, helping put a man on the moon.** I felt like I was building a future, not just for myself, but for the organizations that did business with us, as well as our employees. I sprang out of bed every morning, sometimes after only a couple of hours' sleep, so excited that I had the privilege of waking up to what I was constructing.

There are few benefits in the beginning of starting a company— the hours are thankless and the profits are a long way down the line, so it means everything to have a leader with a vision for what the future will hold. Passion is how we convinced early employees that if we stuck with it, so many of us at the company would be able to live the life of our dreams. The more we believed in us, the more our clients and coworkers did, too. Our company became an ouroboros swallowing its own tail of positivity every time we pushed ourselves and accomplished what none of our competitors could, whether it was completing a million-word translation project or helping the law firm navigate their client's largest-ever bank fine. I wanted to connect the world by creating a company with a foundation in integrity, and it was paying off in every respect.

Words of Wisdom

"Passion will move men beyond themselves, beyond their shortcomings, beyond their failures."

—Joseph Campbell

A Goal Is a Dream with a Deadline

Passion is the first of the Five Ps but without the second P, it's just an inspirational saying that looks cute on a coffee mug. *Prioritization* is the second P because dreams and enthusiasm are not enough; you need solid goals and deadlines. The ability to prioritize is the alchemy that turns those dreams into gold.

Part of our success came from understanding what our priorities were from the beginning. Our mission statement was to become the world's premier and largest language solutions company and we couldn't do that without clients and projects. Like, a lot of them. We had to start producing revenue immediately and that meant hitting the phones and mailing letters in mass on the very first day.

When building a business from scratch, you may feel an inclination to work on the "fun" parts first, such as designing a corporate logo or looking for office space, but without prioritizing generating revenue—absolutely necessary for your company to stay in business—these efforts will be for naught.

Being able to prioritize time requires you to look inside yourself and understand your own productivity because you can't expect your team to be efficient if you yourself aren't. For me, I know I'm happiest when I get an early start, even in my personal life, because I can lose motivation as the day goes on. When I set a goal, I make it the first thing I delve into in the morning, regardless of whether it's working, reading, or exercising. If it's important, I get it out of the way because I know I'll feel better once it's done. I figure out the metrics of whatever it is that I have to accomplish and then I hold myself accountable for completing the task.

Former president of Hearst and author Michael Clinton offers a smart term for prioritization and efficiency in his book *Roar*. He's a proponent of the OHIO concept, which means Only Handle It Once. (My philosophy has always been to touch things only once, but OHIO is far more elegant than TTOO.)

Words of Wisdom

"Do the jobs you like least first. It makes each successive job easier."

—Jim Henson

As you advance in your leadership role, you'll find that you have to delegate some of your decision-making. Regardless of how well you prioritize, it eventually becomes impossible to do it all yourself. **The way to build a company is to make sure you eventually replace yourself; as you grow, you should transition to working *on* the business, rather than *in* the business.** You should create your ideal org chart, revising as needed. I'm a huge fan of what Jeff Bezos calls his "one-way-door" rule that he adopted when he stepped down from his role as CEO of Amazon and began delving into other Amazon initiatives, like Blue Origin and the *Washington Post*.

The rule is that Bezos doesn't need to be involved in any decision that can be reversed, like hiring and laying off workers; those are considered two-way doors because people can always be terminated or rehired. Instead, he should be involved with one-way-door decisions, which are those that cannot be reversed. An example of this would be a company's decision to go public or make an acquisition. Jason Aten wrote about Bezos in his *Inc.* column, saying, "Bezos can't, and shouldn't, be involved in every decision. That was true anyway, but especially if he plans to focus his energy on other things. For Bezos, the one-way-door rule is valuable because it gives him and Amazon a way to decide whether a decision is important enough to get involved. It makes it easier to let go of everything else and focus only on things that have that level of impact on the business. That frees up his time for other things."[5]

The other half of the prioritization equation is prioritizing your expenditures. In the beginning, for every dollar you spend, make **the highest percentage possible go toward sales and marketing, despite the fact that these are not "fun" buys. Above all, this means having the biggest and best sales team in the industry.** Sure, it would look cool if everyone on the team sat comfortably in Aeron chairs at those awesome Restoration Hardware desks made from airplane wings, but these expenditures will not further your company's financial goals. Think of it like this: Everyone wants to buy the vases to display the pretty flowers they've grown, but if they don't first invest in the unglamorous bags of compost and fertilizer, they won't have any flowers to display. This is exactly what Walt Disney meant when he said to stop talking and start doing.

Words of Wisdom

"If it don't make dollars, it don't make sense."

—DJ Quik

Ch-Ch-Changes (Turn and Face the Stranger)

Once you figure out how to prioritize, everything will inevitably change, which brings us to the third P of leading—*pivoting*. The best leaders understand how important it is to be agile, whether they're adjusting to a business shift or addressing a crisis.

One of the biggest crises we faced at our organization was the aftermath of Hurricane Sandy. For those who didn't live on the East Coast, their only exposure to the storm was watching the news and seeing a seemingly unbelievable wall of water pouring down the steps to flood the subway system. Sandy was one of the worst natural disasters to hit the United States. The numbers are staggering—the storm caused $70.2 billion worth of damage, left more than 8 million without power, decimated over 600,000 homes, and killed at least 72 Americans.[6] Our clients had a desperate need to relay a lot of information to a lot of entities, which was all the more difficult because our New York office—our global headquarters—was in the thick of it.

We'd thought we'd prepared for every eventuality after the terrorist attacks in New York but we were mistaken. Our servers went down during Sandy and we lost access to work, problematic because almost all our products and deliverables were stored virtually, a contingency plan we thought was wise to take after 9/11. All my other priorities came to a screeching halt as we decided how to move forward by having other offices pick up New York's workload. We had to figure out everything on the fly. In the aftermath, we created a formal Disaster Recovery team, redundant facilities, and extensive plans for work-from-home protocol in case we ever faced another natural disaster, or dare I say a global pandemic.

Dealing with COVID-19 fallout tested many leaders' mettle. Small businesses like restaurants became the face of the pandemic, as those with one to four employees were the most severely impacted.[7] We all have our favorite dining spots that weathered the virtual storm by getting creative. We actively rooted for them and tried to support them as they set up outdoor seating with heaters and amped up their delivery services. When given the choice to reprioritize or perish, they chose to reprioritize.

Just the Facts

Over 70 percent of small businesses reported a large to moderate negative impact on their businesses from COVID-19.[8]

Of course, larger businesses were hit hard, too, and they also had to pivot. For example, Disney+ decided to release the live-action version of *Mulan* on streaming for an extra fee because they had to find a way to reach audiences who couldn't (or wouldn't) go to a movie theater.

In the summer of 2020, McKinsey & Company surveyed almost 1,000 executives about how their companies transitioned to digital solutions at the height of the stay-at-home order. What's interesting is that the companies surveyed thought the digital transition might take anywhere from nine months to two years, but it took less than a month in most cases. For example, the expected days it would take to increase remote work and collaboration was estimated at 454 days, but in reality, it took 10.5, which is 43 times faster than anticipated.[9] (I hope you bought Zoom stock back then!) Ironically, when asked why they hadn't implemented some of these digital changes earlier, more than half of those surveyed replied that these changes hadn't been a business priority until COVID hit. Necessity has a way of reprioritizing itself.

Words of Wisdom

"Change before you have to."

—Jack Welch

The Opposite of Reactive

The magic happens in the fourth P of leading—*proactivity*, which includes a culture of innovation.

Why do I consider proactivity to be magic? Because when you inspire your people to unleash their creativity, you not only increase employee satisfaction but you can also have a significant impact on your bottom line. In fact, companies where creativity is aligned with corporate culture have a 30 percent higher enterprise value growth and a 17 percent higher profit growth.[10]

But what does it mean to be a company that proactively innovates?

Proactively innovating means not only encouraging employees to come to management with ideas, but to reward them for doing so. I believed in holding innovation contests and we tied raises and promotions to producing new products and services. We did this by fostering an atmosphere where everyone felt comfortable offering suggestions, telling our employees that there were no bad ideas. We encouraged unorthodox thinking and when we were presented with ideas, we figured how we could make them work, rather than shooting them down, saying why they wouldn't.

To promote creativity at Google, the company offers what they call the "20 percent time" rule, which means that employees are encouraged to spend one day a week pursuing whatever their passion might be, because the notion is that having a mental break for playtime actually increases productivity.[11] In fact, it was an employee's passion project that resulted in the Gmail product. Per Google's *Re:Work* blog, "Making innovation part of your organization isn't about starting up a research [and] development lab or focusing your efforts on one set of people. In Google's experience, innovation happens when you make it a valued part of the way people think, work, and interact every day. It's about creating the right environment, hiring the right people, and then getting out of their way."[12]

In the very early stages of my career, I didn't realize that proactivity was critical to being a valuable employee. On my first day of another summer telemarketing job at Moody's, a financial services company, my boss showed me an article he had written. I noticed that the copy had a few minor errors. I wasn't sure what to do. He was going to be on the cover of a magazine and he was proudly showing me the piece, rather than asking for my feedback. The magazine was about to go to print, and of course the smart and right thing for me to have done would have been to immediately notify him of the mistakes. I worried that it would impact our working relationship if I were to tell him what he'd done wrong when he hadn't specifically asked me to proofread it. Being young and naïve, I didn't yet understand that employees need to take ownership of projects. I struggled with whether or not to tell him, but my common sense won out and my boss was grateful for my input. (Had I not done so, that erroneous copy would have haunted me. How could I even have considered letting "They're not doing *they're* best" through?)

What differentiates a good employee from a great one is proactivity, so as a leader, you must encourage this trait. Proactivity is the difference between doing what you're told and asking yourself what else you could be doing, whether it's brainstorming a way to reduce errors or enhancing the clients' experience. For example, my favorite managers were the ones who didn't just send me what I requested, but instead proactively forwarded weekly or monthly updates about their team's numbers and percentage toward goals.

Proactivity means anticipating needs, whether in house or with clients. About 20 years ago, Mark Peeler, a forward-thinking employee of mine, had achieved almost everything he could in his job and was looking to take on a new challenge. He decided to make ours a paperless company, so he took the lead. He changed the way we did business, eliminating tons of paper waste and freeing up acres of square feet of filing space—no small feat when the rent for office space in New York was already running almost $60/per square foot at the time, and is now over $100.

Proactivity means that it's everyone's job to grow the company, and that can take many different shapes. Not coincidentally, our most proactive employees were the ones who earned the most promotions, bonuses, perks, and commissions.

I bet yours are, too.

Everyday People

The fifth P of Leadership can be the easiest facet, as well as the most difficult—*people*. Leadership boils down to getting others to get behind you in the pursuit of a goal. You can be a (somewhat less effective) leader without prioritization or proactivity or the ability to pivot or even passion, but without people, you're just one person being effective all by yourself. Having people who believe in you and your vision is the most important part of being a leader. The caveat is, you must be a person of principle or your vision is just propaganda.

Words of Wisdom

"We learned about honesty and integrity—that the truth matters. . .that you don't take shortcuts or play by your own set of rules. . .and success doesn't count unless you earn it fair and square."

—Michelle Obama

I agree with Google's thinking that once you have the right people, you must get out of their way, but that starts with finding the right people. I specifically hired the kind of people who impressed me, who I thought were smarter than I was. I learned so much from them. Early on, I discovered that my success as a leader, and the company's growth, would stem from having the best people on board. We were incredibly fortunate over the years to have hired so many of them.

Unfortunately, I learned this from my own mistakes of first hiring the *worst* people.

One of my initial employees was a woman we'll call Make-My-Case Colette because whenever she did something that was wrong, rather than accepting constructive criticism and fixing the problem, she spent an inordinate amount of time trying to make the case for her mistake and justify why she did it. And this happened over and over and over. Yes, it was exhausting, thank you for asking. Because we'd started to grow and were desperate for people, I made the mistake of hiring the first candidates I could find. (More on this in Chapter 13.)

For example, she'd answer the phone, "Transparent Transactions," instead of "TransPerfect Translations," mangling the company's name so badly that it threw off every client and prospective client who called.

(And then she'd try to justify the malaprop!) Of course, mistakes do happen, especially initially. I've certainly made and continue to make my share. But it was as though she'd worked at Apple, answered the phone "Banana," and then argued that since they were both fruits it was fine. Making the mistake wasn't the most frustrating part of the situation—the justification was.

I did everything I could to mentor her. She appeared to be immune, however, to my attempts at coaching. The important lesson I learned from this situation is that performance and attitude go hand in hand: Real improvement in performance can be achieved only if performance is accompanied by a positive attitude that allows you to own up to your mistakes and demonstrate a true desire to do better. When a positive attitude does not accompany performance, I'd recommend cutting ties immediately. Make-My-Case Colette was invited to leave, and I made sure her replacement was better.

When I looked for people, I'd reference my experience at Euramerica. I had so much responsibility there but had been frustrated because I had no authority. I knew the constraints of my position so I always felt handicapped in what I could do. That's why I made it my priority to hire those whose values aligned with the company's and encouraged and empowered those people to make decisions without having to ask.

I hired one man who interviewed so well. My first thought was, "This is a person who will go far." We hired him in sales. Initially, his writing was riddled with errors, especially deleterious in an industry where every letter of every word must be correct. (It's the difference between announcing a country's new SDI versus STI.) The feedback I gave him was tough, but he quickly turned it around because he was smart, motivated, and had a fantastic attitude. He ended up being a critical part of our company and one of our top sales leaders. I learned from this experience to always try to right an employee's performance.

My ideal employee was fresh out of college because these people were ready to be molded. I looked for those who were excited about the industry and our company. We found them all the usual ways, from recruiting at colleges to placing ads in the *New York Times* and posting on job boards and, later, LinkedIn. But how we recruited wasn't nearly as important as who we brought on. We wanted those who sought an entrepreneurial experience. Working at the company was a first "real" job for many of our star performers. We found that we had the worst luck when we hired from our competitors, because these people didn't have the same attitude as the new graduates. I'd take attitude, personality, and drive over experience any day of the week.

I found that the best way to lead these teams was to be with them. If they stayed late at the office, I was there with them, making sure we ordered pizza and later thanking them by buying them flowers or a gift card. I believe in recognizing employees by giving comp days and gifts for going above and beyond, and it was important to me that they'd know I'd never ask them to do anything I wouldn't do myself.

My years of interviewing and hiring taught me to offer jobs only to those who shared my core values, which included the notion that it's only arduous work if you'd rather be doing something else. My advice is to create an entire culture of like-minded people, those who want to work hard and play hard, because that will bond you to each other and produce the best results. Of course their skills and their backgrounds should be different and diverse, complementing yours and those of the rest of the team. But their mindset and values should align with yours. Having done this for years at TransPerfect, I saw an awful lot of friendships form. We even had many marriages!

This philosophy extends to when you make acquisitions. Make sure your company culture aligns with that of the company you're acquiring. If it doesn't, the merger is likely to be a disaster.

One way to increase your team's loyalty is to pay better than any of your competitors. For example, many companies limit commission, which is a terrible idea. When you limit compensation, people stop performing. Why put in 150 percent when you're only going to be paid for doing 100 percent? As your sales reps make more money, encourage them to expand their teams and divide some of their spoils as they scale. This will lead to this greater gains both for your people and for the company.

When giving bonuses to your production teams, do so based on their percent of revenue and profit, and not just across the board; this will attract the greatest talent. Incentives should always align with performance, rather than tenure.

However, it's not enough just to lead people by financial incentives because that creates mercenaries. It can't just be about dollars, or else they'll jump ship the second someone else pays a few extra bucks. People need more than that, and you'll learn what specifically they need through your one-on-one time. My philosophy entails lifelong growth and advancement. If possible, structure your company so that there is always another level your employees can reach. Be generous with titles and creative with career paths.

Employees want to know that they're doing an excellent job and it was important for me to acknowledge their hard work, not just in compensation, but also public recognition, whether in a speech to fellow employees or an email to the company. I'd talk about who was doing a fantastic job and I'd give specifics on why they should be emulated. It's been said that public recognition is three times more impactful than private recognition. This works well for motivating their coworkers and clearly delineating what they should be doing as well. If there was ever negative feedback, I'd do it in private, and would always buffer what was wrong with what was going right.

What I miss most about the company is our employees. Fortunately, through my mentoring and charitable work, I'm still able to work with many fantastic people.

The difference is now I'm not building a dream company. Instead, I'm focused on building a dream world.

Remember, you don't need to be the boss to be a leader (but you do need to have iron-clad ethics). Whether you're a Henson or a Welch, your leadership style will be far more effective if you embrace the Five Ps.

Words of Wisdom

"Before you are a leader, success is all about growing yourself. When you become a leader, success is all about growing others."

—Jack Welch

12

Servicing

When I used to speak about servicing, it was about spoiling or "wowing" the client with service, terms I used consistently for more than 25 years. However, I learned over time that servicing—and in the process, retaining—your employees, is just as important. It's been said that if you take care of your employees, they will take care of your clients, and your business will take care of itself.

You may have the most competent employees in the business, but if you're not actively working to retain those people, you're going to lose a lot of time, money, and market share. In the previous chapter, we covered the notion that you're not a leader without people. In this chapter, we'll get into exactly what it takes to *keep* your people, and that process begins and ends with service.

Words of Wisdom

"Whoever renders service to many puts himself in line for greatness—great wealth, great return, great satisfaction, great reputation, and great joy."

—Jim Rohn

Service Begins on Day One

The thing about a first impression is that you have only one chance to make it. That's why my goal was to give my employees a fantastic first day on the job. Many of us have worked at that one place where we've shown up and it's clear that the boss forgot we were starting that day. There's little more awkward or off-putting than standing around in a scratchy new business suit while our manager tries to scrounge up a spare chair and a folding table to park us in temporarily, then waiting hours—or days—for network access.

My suggestion is that you avoid that terrible impression, instead setting up every new hire for success. Before your new employee ever walks into the office, be ready for them. Have their workspace arranged at a real desk and not just some chair you dragged in from the reception area. Have their computer ready with all their access and permissions in place. Stock their office supplies and print their business cards because the second most awkward interaction is having to write your contact info on the back of an envelope because you don't yet have your cards.

At TransPerfect, I'd do a CEO lunch so I could get to know the new person because I wanted to stress that they belonged with the company. I believe the time to find out about your new people begins as soon as they start. So, at our lunch, we'd discuss their passions, their hobbies, their families—whatever they loved. I'd find out how they liked to work and when they felt most effective during their day so we could set them up for success. For example, with me, it's mornings all the way, so I wouldn't have thrived on a second or third shift. (I would be a terrible vampire; I'd have never made it to upper management.)

The more we knew those onboarding, the more welcome they'd feel and the better we could find ways to motivate them for peak performance. Through servicing, the employer is always trying to inspire the employee to do more, whether it's more sales, more creativity, or more loyalty. I was a fan of throwing a first-day get-together for our new team members to show them how much we appreciated their joining us. **I find it ironic that companies wait to give their employees a cake at the end when they're quitting—it's too late, and losing someone is nothing to celebrate.**

Just the Facts

According to the Society for Human Resource Management, the hard cost per new hire is $4,700. However, factoring in the soft costs such as time invested in the search and loss of productivity, the total hard and soft costs of recruiting can run as much as three times the employee's salary.[1]

Please Don't Go

Given those hard and soft costs, it's almost always preferable to keep current staff, which is why I recommend the use of stay interviews. These cover the same sort of material we'd ask during an exit interview. Only instead of saying, "What didn't you like about the work environment?" the questions are posed in the present tense. **I believe the most important question you can ask is, "What would you do differently if you owned the company?"** The employees' answers in the stay interview are used to retain people (as well as improve the company), proactively fixing problems, rather than conducting a postmortem on why they left. No one wants to be the sad boyfriend of a company, crying, "I can change!" as they chase after the employee who got away.

My philosophy is to create an environment where people want to stay and grow with the company, which is easy to assess if you're conducting one-on-on and skip-level meetings. If you're perpetually soliciting feedback, you're perpetually in the know. I understand there's an inclination for managers to forgo these meetings because they're busy and the meetings take time, but those managers will be far busier if they lose key staff members over fixable issues.

While compensation is always important in retaining employees, and we'll discuss this more soon, it's not everything. People are motivated by personal development and learning, so we created teaching modules on skills like negotiation techniques, leadership, proofreading, and the like. We added the kind of perks, such as trips, wheelspins, and bonuses, that made people want to stick around.

It was important to me to be a part of the interview process for many years for a couple of reasons. Let's start with the fact that people are more invested in the company when they see that senior management is interested and invested in *them*. (And I really was!) I used to say that we weren't just hiring people for one job—we were hiring them for three jobs from now or the next 20 years. I looked for potential hires who could, with development, training, patience, and discipline, handle a position multiple levels up. Our company had an outstanding record for promotion because we hired people who were forward-thinking. Ironically, we often struggled to keep the reception position filled because we brought on people hungry to advance.

The View from the Top

Every business starts small. TransPerfect was a twist on the common refrain of companies that started in a garage, having begun in a dorm room. When Meg Whitman took the job at eBay in 1998, the company had 30 employees, just enough to fill a bus. She believed in the founder's vision, so she accepted the position as president and CEO. She credits the growth of the company—which now employs more than 10,000 people, enough to fill an arena—to the notion of providing what she called a "career adventure," meaning plenty of room to grow and advance. She's also spoken about hiring "ahead of the curve," so she would look for employees who could handle a job that was bigger than what they were hired for initially; that way, the employee and the company could grow in tandem.[2]

The notion of providing career paths is common in the best companies. For example, take Amazon. They're investing $1.2 billion in their Career Choice Program, which includes fully funded college education at hundreds of accredited colleges and universities. This program prepays tuition, books, and fees with no lifetime limit and is available to all 750,000 of its employees after only 90 days of employment.[3]

In some organizations, the opportunity for career development begins before their potential employees even enter the workforce. For example, Adobe recruits not only on college campuses but also via coding clubs, helping those candidates build their skills and experience through internships.[4]

If providing a career path paved with training and development opportunities weren't important, then it's not something so many leading employers would offer.

But how do you service someone who *isn't* looking for education and advancement?

To answer that, I'll take us back to my time at Euramerica.

Large and in Charge

I thought Euramerica was my dream company the first time I walked into their offices at 21st and Park. I already loved the idea of working with languages, but when I saw the workspace, I was completely bowled over. This was 1987, and we'd barely scratched the surface of the need for personal computers. But at Euramerica, the walls were glass and every workstation had a Macintosh computer on it. I felt like I was in *The Jetsons*.

The company didn't have any open sales positions, so I took a job in production. I made my mark by trying to outwork my peers and adding value to the position. Once I finished my tasks, I'd be an *intrapreneur*, always looking for things to do outside of my job description. For example, I noticed we were losing time getting quotes back to clients, so I created guidelines for giving rates.

Based on my own experience, my advice to new employees is that if you're at the beginning of your career and you don't stick with it and do what it takes to make your mark, you'll be left behind. Paying your dues will never go out of style, so I always tell those who are starting out that it's imperative never to act like you're above doing the grunt work.

The whole time I was in production, I had my eye on sales. I wanted to crush it so when the opportunity arose, I'd have established my bona fides. After a year at the company, I looked at everything I'd been doing, specifically at how my ideas, recommendations, and contributions had benefited the company. Given my performance, I believed I should be paid more, but I knew that nothing would happen if I didn't ask.

Liz's Life Lesson

No one can toot your own horn like you can.

I presented my case for a raise and a promotion, highlighting the numbers I'd achieved. I gave solid examples of all the things I'd done, my KPIs, the number of projects I'd completed, and both the revenue of the projects, as well as the profit margins.

I successfully presented my rationale, receiving not only a healthy bump in my salary, but a promotion. . .and an employee to manage. At 22 years old, I suddenly found myself in charge of a 50-something British man named Brian. He was a career editor, not looking to scale the corporate ladder. Even though he didn't want the job I got, I can't imagine he was thrilled by suddenly having to report to someone young enough to be his daughter. He was a talented linguist and an excellent editor, so I had to figure out not only how to work with him, but also how to keep him happy in his role.

Even if I found a better way for him to do his job, I lacked the credibility to try to shape or mold him; he'd been editing longer than I'd been alive. The way I kept him happy and motivated was not to try to change him. Instead, I took the approach of being respectful. I made everything about results and I worked closely with him to come up with ways that I could serve him, making it easier for him to meet his goals.

As a result, our department exceeded our metrics and I was promoted again, this time into sales.

Words of Wisdom

"The best way to find yourself is to lose yourself in the service of others."

—Mahatma Gandhi

Take It Personally

To service my employees, I would build on what I learned about them on the first day, always trying to find out what inspired and motivated them. I strongly recommend that you take the time to learn who your employees are as individuals, with full lives outside of the work arena. The more you understand the *why* of your employees' behavior, the better you can accommodate them. For example, let's say you have a motivated worker who's consistently exceeded their production goals, but suddenly you see their numbers tapering. The shortcut would be to issue a warning and put them on a probationary plan to improve. But that doesn't get to the root of why your rock star is suddenly singing the blues.

A one-on-one will often reveal what's going on in their lives, and if you dig a bit, you'll discover the root of the problem. Perhaps you'll find out that the employee is distracted by a sick child or an ailing parent; then you can accommodate that employee with a more flexible work schedule, and they'll be back in tune in no time.

Theodore Roosevelt once said, "Nobody cares how much you know until they know how much you care," and this is a quote I've always taken to heart. It's crucial to have a relationship with your employees, not treating them like a cog in the machine. Everyone who works for you is a living, breathing, sentient human being who worries about their health, family, and career. The more you recognize that, the more you can connect with them. And the more you connect, the better they'll perform. Generally, people don't quit a company, they quit a boss. I took every employee's decision to leave personally, so I strived to be the person they didn't want to quit.

Let's Get Engaged

If you want to retain your people, it's important to have your employees engage. Engagement means an employee has enthusiasm about their jobs and they're committed to the workplace. Compensation is one way of promoting this, but again, if there aren't other methods in play, you run the risk of creating mercenaries who are loyal to their paychecks and not to the company. Employee engagement makes companies more successful, as according to SMARP, an employee engagement and communications platform, "Engaged employees outperform their peers that are not engaged. Overall, companies with high employee engagement are 21 percent more profitable."[5]

Sounds great, right? But how the heck do you get them to engage?

Well, let's look at how CarMax did it. In 2008 when everything began to crash and burn, employees everywhere were worried about being downsized, or at the very least losing perks and benefits. However, CEO Tom Folliard wanted to make those hard times easier on his employees, so he had the company invest more in employee training and development programs, which enabled his people to get raises and promotions. He also rewarded employees for being creative and submitting ideas that would benefit the company and its customers, actively getting them to engage more in how their company was run. (Ahem, sound familiar?) At the Great Place to Work conference in 2012, Folliard said of his programs, "Take care of your associates, they will take care of our customers, and the rest will take care of itself."[6]

Charles Schwab has employed a different but equally successful approach. Schwab management recognized that their employees would be more engaged in the workplace if they were to treat their employees to the same kind of sound financial advice that they gave to their clients. So Schwab began to offer free financial consultation and workshops, and they started supplementing their 401(k) matching system with rewards that came from their employee recognition program.[7] Being engaged at Schwab paid off, literally.

There are countless ways to encourage employee engagement. L'Oréal launched the Fit Culture App in 2017, to help onboard and support their new employees. Available in 11 different languages, the Fit Culture App is meant to be a fun and easy way for newbies to learn about the company, with info presented in bite-sized capsules so it's never onerous, including lessons, anecdotes, and corporate legends. Per L'Oréal's Director of International Learning Practice Laurent Reich, "Our objective with the Fit Culture App is to take our onboarding practices to the next level and to give each and every employee, from the moment they arrive, the keys to succeed in full alignment with company values such as multiculturalism, diversity and inclusion."[8]

What I like about the idea of Fit Culture is the value it provides in giving a consistent message about the company's history and culture. However, I believe that it's necessary to make sure that they supplement the app with in-person training on the company's culture and vision. The personal touch is critical to optimize morale and ensure that people feel a part of the team. Still, I love thinking that if there are inside jokes at L'Oréal, everyone's included in learning about them via the app—because they believe their employees are worth it.

Of course, the notion of employee engagement has been made far more challenging in the post-COVID workplace, thanks to the Great Resignation. In fact, more than 4.5 million workers walked away from their jobs in one month of 2021.[9] What's making the difference between a labor force on the verge of packing it up and happy employees are those employers who recognize that there's no going back to the old ways. To thrive, employers must offer more flexibility, opportunities for remote work, and a conscious effort to focus on their employees' mental health. We can't play by the rules that worked prior to 2020 anymore.

Despite your best efforts, understand that there will always be employees who resign because they want to become entrepreneurs. Some of our top people eventually left—despite their level of engagement—to start their own companies.

And I couldn't be happier for and more proud of them.

Just the Facts

Thirty-four percent of employees were considered "engaged" with their work in 2022, meaning enthusiastic about and committed to their workplace, which is up from a low of 13 percent in 2013.[10]

Show Me the Money

Regardless of a company's most sincere intentions to engage and serve their employees, a candidate's decision on whether to take the job will hinge on compensation because they can't pay their mortgage with atta-boys or atta-girls. So let's unpack how to pay people.

I firmly believe a salesperson's comp should be unlimited. The moment a company puts a cap on earnings is the moment that performer activates their job search on LinkedIn. That said, I don't advocate for high base salaries for sales because that takes away their incentive. My recommendation is to keep the draw (meaning the advance on future commissions in a down month) as low as possible in order to keep them hungry (and prevent complacency) but offer that unlimited upside with commissions. Any salesperson who balks at not having the safety of a large draw is not the person you want to hire.

Eventually, we did roll out a relationship management position because we realized we had high-caliber employees who had a depth of knowledge we valued and were more suited to and interested in being farmers than hunters. Due to the depth and breadth of what they knew, these hybrid sales positions were crucial in helping us retain and grow clients.

If you want to incentivize your sales team to keep their clients, implement non-sunset commissions, meaning pay the same percentage commission on long-term clients as on brand-new clients. When sales is always paid on this business, it keeps them motivated to remain in constant touch with their clients. I also believe production teams should be paid the same percentage on long-term clients as on new business, so they are at least as motivated to work their existing accounts. This is key, because it can cost anywhere from 5 to 25 times more to attract a new client than retain a current one.[11] **Virtually all long-term sustainable growth results from repeat business and referrals.**

You may have little other choice in the beginning, so I recommend not paying commission until the client pays their invoice. Instead, pay on payments the company has received. My philosophy is that it's not enough to sell the project, but also to ensure the company is paid on the work completed. The best way to do this is to have the sales team ultimately responsible for collections and offer inducements for quick payment. While I wouldn't say you want a sales team to hound your clients like the iconic psychotic paperboy in the movie *Better Off Dead*, I wouldn't say you don't either. No one wants clients who try to skate out of their financial responsibilities.

At Euramerica, I had always felt as though sales and production were on separate teams. They were constantly at odds with one another and measured by different metrics. They weren't a one-firm firm, which meant departments could work against each other. This didn't produce the most positive client experience. Departments should be competing against themselves, not others within the company. I believed everything would work better if sales and production were on the same team, so that's how I wanted to set things up. I quantified production's performance based on the numbers and gave them the opportunity to earn more based on profit margin. But after we really got rolling, we realized we needed to give production the same types of perks that sales had, including benefits like Platinum Club. Everyone benefited from the trips we awarded, the education we offered, and the speakers we brought in, including luminaries from Colin Powell to Coach K.

If you make sure that yours is the most competitive compensation, you won't lose your best people to the competition.

Words of Wisdom

"Opportunity is missed by most people because it is dressed in overalls and looks like work."

—Thomas Edison

Understanding how to service employees is a must for any organization looking to grow and remain competitive.

The bottom line is that the more your company gives your people, the more you'll get back from them.

Words of Wisdom

"Realize that employees and the customers both have to be engaged, at the same time, to move your business forward for sustainable success."

—Robert G. Thompson

13

Hiring

I attribute virtually all of my success to having hired great people and then getting out of their way. Employees can make or break your business, so if you want to grow, it's crucial to have the kind of people who'll have your company's back. I'm a firm believer that if you bring in the best people, they will take you to the top.

So let's delve into strategies for determining who can help your organization ascend to the next level.

Words of Wisdom

"Start with good people, lay out the rules, communicate with your employees, motivate and reward them. If you do all these things effectively, you can't miss."

—Lee Iacocca

Patience, Grasshopper

When I was first beginning as an entrepreneur, I didn't know how much I didn't know in regard to hiring. Most of my learning was of the seat-of-my-pants variety and I made many mistakes. While ethics were important to me from day one, I hadn't yet learned what else might be important, because ethical doesn't necessarily mean motivated. There are plenty of fine individuals who are perfectly satisfied with the status quo.

Our first few employees were a comedy of errors, from No-Touch-Trash Tamara to Make-My-Case Colette. Here's where we went wrong with hiring in the early days. We had burned ourselves out by working so many 100-hour weeks, trying to get some traction in the industry. We had been successful in landing business, but we were still grinding so hard that we didn't have the effort to put into our hiring process; we were afraid that would take away from our focus on sales.

The thing about desperation (mixed with exhaustion) is that it doesn't lead to the best decision-making. We needed people so badly that we settled for the first ones who walked in the door, convincing ourselves that they could do the job, when no part of their interview answers should have led us to that conclusion. That's when I learned **the most important piece of advice there is regarding employees, which comes from my mentor, Jack Daly: Hire slowly, fire quickly.** (More on that shortly.) We lost a lot of ground in the beginning because we'd staffed up so poorly.

We should have waited for the rock stars who we could see with us 5 to 10 years down the line, but we were too overwhelmed and over-tired to employ that kind of patience. Great people were hard to find, and back in the mid-1990s, no one was excited to work for a startup, especially given the low draw in sales and crazy hours in production. The dot-com boom was on the horizon, but we were still in the nascent days, so there wasn't the excitement or cachet of working on the ground floor of a startup. No one had gotten beyond-their-wildest-dreams-rich after their startup had been acquired by Google or Facebook yet—neither entity existed.

While we offered unlimited commissions to our sales teams and bonuses to our rock stars in production, the people we brought in were working such grueling hours that eventually the money wasn't worth it to them and we'd lose them. Our job in the early days with staffing was trying to maintain that sweet spot between hungry and burned out.

Tell Me a Little Bit About Yourself

Over the years, I developed a much better sense of who would be the right fit for our team. One of the first assumptions I had to get past was that the best employees would come from Ivy League schools. While I was always impressed with the kind of education that came with a degree from places like Harvard, Yale, and Princeton, the Ivies didn't necessarily churn out people who were hungry to be successful in sales or production roles, at least at our company. These kids were often less willing to go out of their way to drum up business or innovate and they had the wrong attitude. In my experience, they often didn't want to pay their dues, having assumed that obligation had been satisfied through their tuition payments and the performance that had gotten them accepted initially. Their performance had literally peaked in school. The longer I hired people, the less correlation I saw between prestigious schools and success within the company.

I interviewed every single employee myself until we were a 100-person company and many more over the years. **Once I'd gotten into the groove of hiring, I discovered that attitude was just as important as experience.** I'd seek out those who impressed me, those who thought big. I wanted those looking for a company where they could grow and where they had a stake in growing the company. I wanted them to be able to envision themselves three positions up, ten years in the future. I appreciated those who came prepared with lists of questions, not just about the company, but also about me and my experience, because it showed ambition and a natural curiosity. I wanted to see people who'd make the effort, so I was less impressed with those who wanted to know about information readily available on the first page of our website. If nothing else, at least read the landing page! I figured if they weren't willing to make the effort for a conversation with me, why would I believe they'd do it with our clients?

Given the choice, I'd opt for someone with skills over experience, a practice favored by Sheryl Sandberg that she learned from Meg Whitman. When Sandberg interviewed at eBay, she was completely honest with Whitman, saying she'd lacked experience in the tech world, a fact that had gotten her summarily rejected by a number of tech companies. (Imagine being the hiring manager who passed on Sheryl Sandberg! That must have felt like all those editors who didn't see any potential in the first Harry Potter book.)

In an interview with Reid Hoffman, LinkedIn's cofounder, Sandberg said, "[Meg] said 'no one has any experience, because no one has ever done this before. I want to hire people with great skills, and I think hopefully you have great skills.' I really took that lesson to heart.... I decided what mattered was skills. I was going to go hire the best and the brightest, and people who were going to bring their passion and dedication and work hard. And actual experience in the field or related fields didn't matter. That opens up a lot of hiring, because then you can just look for skills."[1]

My ideal employee was someone with integrity who also was incredibly service oriented. I particularly liked those who'd been in sports because athletics promotes leadership, a competitive drive, and teamwork. Winning was important to them. I appreciated those who'd waited tables in bars and restaurants because they'd seen people at their worst and had learned to navigate difficult situations with diplomacy. (Few skills will get you better equipped for how rough the world can be than managing the Saturday night dinner rush.) I favored those who came out of college with student loans because those who hadn't had everything paid for were hungrier. And those who'd encountered adversity were more resilient. I sought out enthusiasm, energy, and a track record of success.

One of my favorite employees started in the early days, and what blew me away was his can-do attitude. Jamie Wengroff was perpetually cheerful and upbeat and could not do enough for his clients. He used to walk around the office saying, "If it's to be, it's up to me." He set the standard for the kind of person we wanted to hire.

Words of Wisdom

"Hospitality is almost impossible to teach. It's all about hiring the right people."

—Danny Meyer

Sometimes applicants were phenomenal on paper but did poorly in the interviews. I believed that both eye contact and a decent handshake were important and lacking either left me with a poor impression. I was tough in the interviews and had specific expectations. If someone came in and gave answers that didn't align with what they had written on their CV, I'd pass on them. Dressed unprofessionally? Pass. Job hopper? Pass. If someone presented with low energy, negativity, or no questions? Pasadena.

Please don't even get me started on the college grads who *brought their parents with them to the interview, or, worse, had their folks follow up with me.*

I wish I was kidding.

Liz's Life Lesson

Wait until you get to the lobby to call your mom.

If potential employees made it through our gauntlet, we gave them a proofreading or writing test before we hired them. We even did this for our potential sales team members because they'd be responsible for so much written communication with clients, from proposals to letters. (Side note: I always found it interesting that the Ivy League grads were no better and often worse at proofreading than those from state schools.)

For everyone who says cover letters don't matter, I beg to differ. They were important to me and I used them to gauge interest level and writing skills. I'd eliminated anyone with typos on their résumé because mistakes were an indicator of their attention to detail and, thus, future success in the company. I also favored those who'd had lots of paid experience. I sought out those who'd worked their way through school because that told me they were hungry and could attain balance.

I've encountered entrepreneurs whose businesses have never grown bigger than a couple of million in revenue per year. While that kind of money is nothing to sneeze at, these companies have never experienced stratospheric growth.

There are a couple of reasons for this. First, the founders have been reluctant to stop trying to handle all the sales themselves. I know from personal experience how hard it is to let go, but for the sake of growth, it's necessary. They don't hire enough salespeople. They can't become a billion-dollar business with only a few pairs of boots on the ground. In addition to bringing on more salespeople, they should consider bringing in outside partners to sell to their clients, giving them a shared percentage of the profit. I brought in one of my earliest big clients, Toyo Information Systems, through a partner.

However, if you want a premier sales team and more growth than you dreamed possible, you must build it and compensate accordingly. A skilled salesperson will always more than pay for themselves. These small companies also often default to hiring people already established in the industry, assuming that will give them a leg up, but this approach is too limiting in my opinion. While experience is important, it's not everything. I rarely hired those who were career translation people; instead, I opted for those with ambition, knowing that we could teach them our ways.

I knew that we could train and develop anyone with the right attitude, so training and development became a cornerstone of our company. We created a lot of successful leaders from people who began at the entry level.

The Good News Is You're Fired

Earlier I mentioned my interview question about working in an ice cream shop and what would happen if the interviewee witnessed someone stealing from the cash register. I asked every single person I ever hired this question because it showed me not only that the person would take ownership, but also that they had integrity.

Hiring people with integrity is not optional; it's a must. **You not only need them to be an honest steward of your business, but you also want them to have enough integrity to be honest with *you*.** Hard as you might try, there will be times in the boardroom when it will feel easier for your team to just go along, to rubber-stamp your decisions, but that's when it's imperative that they level with you. There must be transparency that goes both ways and that compels your people to give you all the news, *even if it's not what you want to hear*. Having employees with enough integrity to share a harsh truth could be the difference between a successful Dove bodywash campaign and one that sets the internet on fire because of the inadvertent racial implications.

Words of Wisdom

"It's not the employees you don't hire who give you ulcers; it's the ones you do."

—Jack Daly

One dishonest person can throw your whole company off its axle. For example, we brought on a highly skilled person to run an office in South America. Because we were in an entirely different country and couldn't be hands-on, much of the business was run on the honor system. We knew if we wanted to grow, we had to be able to delegate, so it was a calculated risk every time we opened a new office.

Regardless of how thoroughly we screened the new manager and how well he'd interviewed, it turned out that we'd brought on a person who couldn't be trusted. While we were correct in assessing that he'd be a skilled salesman, it didn't occur to us that he was selling his own services instead of ours. He'd used our company name and reputation to get projects, and then would funnel all the revenues into his own pocket. We lost a lot of time, money, and credibility trying to right that situation.

In another case, after many years of struggling to find a CFO, and signing every single check myself, we finally hired our first one. Unfortunately, we soon discovered he was stealing money by forging company checks to his friends and relatives. In this case, of course, we immediately terminated him. And I then went back to signing every check myself. Woo-hoo!

I always say you don't have a mouse, you have mice, and the same is true when you allow a dishonest person to remain in your organization. Sometimes it's not even a matter of theft. For example, we caught one person falsifying certification documents, not because it gave them personal gain, but because it was faster and easier.

In another situation, an employee I knew outside of work quit our organization and I asked to read her exit interview. An HR manager gave it to me and as I read, I was completely confused. Nothing in the interview aligned with what I knew to be true from our relationship outside of the workplace. Instead of admitting making the mistake and confessing that there was no interview, the HR manager had *literally forged the entire exit interview*. This was back in the days that they were handwritten. The manager had made up the answers, which was a thousand times worse.

After these experiences, I learned that we needed to start requiring every single new hire to pass a complete background check before their first day. We immediately incorporated that step into our hiring process.

While my advice is to fire quickly in certain cases, it's never done without cause. In the case where you have an employee struggling with performance, it's necessary to give them feedback in an attempt to right the ship. Give them specifics, both written and in person. Make it clear what's gone wrong, and provide a path to quick improvement. You've invested in them, so you don't want to lose them over something you can coach them through.

Despite your best efforts, sometimes you'll find yourself with the wrong person in the wrong job. Something I'd always say in one-on-ones was that I would never fire an employee out of the blue (assuming it's not due to an integrity issue), so I'd ask that they'd never quit out of the blue. They should communicate their issues and you, as a manager, should do the same. Often the situation can be rectified. If they can't be moved to a different position where they can make the most of their skills, it may be time to cut them loose. The thing about firing is that it should never be a surprise because there have been systematic warnings every step of the way. If you must fire someone, don't make it personal; focus solely on the business parameters that weren't met.

Remember that performance can be rehabbed, but attitude and values can't. If attitude or values is the stumbling block, this is what I mean by fire fast. Whenever we had to let someone go, we'd have an extensive paper trail leading up to the firing and we'd do it in the company of a representative from human resources. After, we'd walk them out the door.

What no one tells you is that—regardless of how justified you are—firing is never an easy endeavor. No one wants to be on the giving or especially the receiving end of what is ultimately a failure. My advice is to take the time to determine if you're hiring the right person, regardless of how pressed you feel to bring someone in.

There are a couple of ways to keep yourself from having to hire too quickly. Have patience, but also have a pipeline. If you're in a pinch, bring in contract employees to fill the gap. In a tight labor market, you always have to have an eye on recruitment so you're never in the position to settle for someone who isn't your first choice. If you can, give that person a trial run of a week or two before making a formal decision. While you may lose someone you thought could have been great, you're saving yourself a lot of hassle on the back end.

Just the Facts

73 percent of potential candidates are passive job seekers, meaning they're not actively looking to change their employment, which is why it's key for employers to maintain that pipeline.[2]

I Love You, You're Perfect, Never Change

My ideal employee had specific traits. That person would always know exactly where they were in relation to their goal, and they'd have a clear directive of what they'd do to achieve the desired results. They were go-getters who appreciated our corporate culture and consistently exceeded my expectations. Their learning curve would be low. Our star performers were promoted from within whenever possible, so it lent credibility to those they now supervised, as they'd previously done their employees' jobs.

We'd normally promote people from within a peer group, which was rarely problematic as it was always based on the numbers or other quantifiable results. Here's the thing with our numbers—everyone knew them. Our management reports were widely shared and we'd post them in public areas, as well as on screens and monitors. Because everyone could see where they were in comparison, this practice changed the space and made people go-getters. Everyone saw that those who were getting the best results got the most recognition and it made people think, *This could happen for me, too.* (Or sometimes, *I'm falling behind and maybe I should shop for shoes on my own time in the future.*)

Two of these rock stars were sales leaders, Colleen Chulis and Matt Mores. They were extremely goal oriented, extraordinarily proactive, personified the highest level of service, and exemplified integrity. As a result, they were each consistently our top sales performers and incredibly inspirational leaders of their respective teams.

Wharton School of Business professor Martin Bidwell looked at the 30-year trend of workers leapfrogging from one company to another, hypothesizing that employers didn't understand how much more expensive it was to bring in new people, rather than promote from within. Bidwell discovered that while external hires were brought in at a higher salary, they tended to rank lower in their performance reviews—significantly so—and thus were more likely to get laid off than those promoted from within.

New usually wasn't better.

In a *Forbes* article about this study, Susan Adams writes, "The external hires made 18% more than the internal promotes in the same jobs. In addition to scoring worse on performance reviews, external hires were 61% more likely to be fired from their new jobs than were those who had been promoted from within the firm. The external hires tended to have more education and experience than the internal hires, but Bidwell says employers don't appreciate how important it is for workers to know the ropes of an organization."[3]

Words of Wisdom

"People don't get promoted for doing their jobs really well. They get promoted for their potential to do more."

—Tara Jaye Frank

Diversify Yourself

My father was an early proponent for equality. I grew up having been taught that a woman could do anything. My dad's motto was to hire the best person for the job. When he was the president of the Canadian division of Grey Advertising, 50 percent of his direct reports were female at a time when this was far from the norm.

It goes without saying that every company should have a plan for diversity recruitment, actively seeking out those from diverse backgrounds, including cultural, racial, gender, age, religion, and physical diversity, not just because it's the right thing to do, but because it's critical for the company's bottom line.

Just the Facts

Diverse and inclusive companies outperform their competition by 35 percent.[4] Diverse companies are 70 percent more likely to capture new markets.[5] Teams that are diverse are 87 percent better at making decisions.[6] And two out of every three job seekers are looking for companies with a diverse workforce.[7]

When healthcare giant Johnson & Johnson made the commitment to embrace diversity, they did so by creating a "Diversity University." This program gives employees the tools they need to create an inclusive workplace, teaching skills such as how to recognize unconscious bias. They've reaped the benefits of their billion-dollar program, with an uptick of 27 percent more employee retention, engagement by 43 percent, and customer retention by 58 percent. Thanks to these efforts, they continually show up on the Best Places to Work list for working mothers and for those with disabilities.

Having representation in senior management will help prevent your company from making an expensive and embarrassing faux pas, like when the brand Popchips decided to make an ad with Ashton

Kutcher in brownface, having him play the role of Raj, an Indian Bollywood producer on a dating website. Did the promo go exactly as poorly as you might imagine, because *brownface*? Yes. Yes, it did. The worst part is, the company at first tried to defend the ad, saying it was supposed to be lighthearted and fun. After the backlash, the company changed its position and pulled the ad after issuing an apology, but that's a bell that's hard to un-ring.

What can be even worse is when an organization touts diversity but doesn't follow through in practice. Take the example of State Street Global Advisors, the investment firm that commissioned the Fearless Girl bronze statue that depicts a little girl staring down a snarling Wall Street bull. The reason behind the commission was that it was a way for State Street to pressure companies to have more female representation on their boards. What's embarrassing is that a few months after the statue went up, State Street had to pay a $5 million claim by the US Department of Labor because it had been determined that State Street had systematically discriminated against women and Black employees through unequal pay.[8] A commitment to diverse hiring must be more than just window dressing. Or bronze statues.

I saw a need for diversity hiring at TransPerfect, at every level, as long as the person we were recruiting was as good or better than the job required. I talked about this recently in *Forbes*, where I said, in effect, that naysayers would have you believe that diversity hiring by definition results in *unqualified* candidates taking positions away from *qualified* ones (a belief that typically comes with assumptions about what exactly a qualified candidate looks like—and who doesn't fit the part). I noted that the merest presence of diversity in an office, on screen, on the ballot, or really in a position with any visibility can result in accusations that affirmative action has unfairly tipped the scales and handed out something that wasn't *deserved*. I believe strongly that the evidence suggests that having a wealth of diversity in the boardroom not only makes a company more successful, but also has a meaningful, lasting impact on working conditions for every employee, with a focus on hiring qualified women working as a "conduit to women's leadership." In other words, diversity and inclusion in hiring actually *works*—quite well, in fact. They can help jump-start not only more inclusive hiring, but also create a more equitable, healthy company culture, positively impact attitudes toward diversity, and ultimately strengthen recruitment and employee retention and, in turn, foster more diverse leadership (all while making companies more profitable and innovative).[9]

The most innovative, profitable companies consider diversity recruiting a core value, and they have the employee retention to prove it. That's why I cannot urge you strongly enough to embrace diversity.

Words of Wisdom

"A diverse mix of voices leads to better discussions, decisions, and outcomes for everyone."

—Sundar Pichai

Organizations aren't nameless, faceless entities; they are comprised of people. And the more skilled and content those people are, the more that company will grow. That's why a company's success begins with finding the right person.

Words of Wisdom

"In looking for people to hire, you look for three qualities: integrity, intelligence, and energy. If they don't have the first, the other two will kill you."

—Warren Buffett

IV

Reinventing the Win

14

Pivoting

No matter how hard you try, no matter how diligently you plan and set goals, a time will come when things change and you'll require the agility to switch to a Plan B.

That you must course-correct isn't what defines you or your company. The ability to pivot is not only one of the Five Ps of Leadership, but also what separates the women from the girls and the men from the boys. Pivoting is how you rebuild and how you rebound, stronger than before.

Words of Wisdom

"A pivot is a change in strategy without a change in vision."

—Eric Ries

Netflix and Chill

Some of the biggest companies today still exist because they changed the way they conducted their business, embracing the pivot. For example, look at Netflix. In the beginning, Netflix was a mail-order DVD service. Users would create a queue of movies and TV shows they wanted to watch. After the consumer viewed their media (or, after, say *50 First Dates* sat unwatched on their coffee table for a month), they'd mail it back in a prepaid envelope and as soon as the post office scanned the barcode on the envelope, the next available disc in the queue would then ship. Netflix didn't even wait for the discs to get back to their facility, so viewers weren't impacted by slow mail delivery. Their business model provided an alternative to having to leave the house to hit the crapshoot of what might be available at Blockbuster. The real draw was that there wasn't a time limit on how long you could hold onto a disc, so you'd never accrue late fees.

Netflix stayed abreast of changes in the industry and when they saw the move to streaming, they knew how this might impact their bottom line. So they asked themselves: Why would consumers want to wait for the mail when they could instead click a button and see whatever they wanted, whenever they wanted? Netflix gambled on how people would consume their media and they opted to invest in the streaming option, obviously the wise choice. Then they pivoted even more to offer up original programming. Netflix has now become so iconic and part of our collective experience that it's almost impossible to recall the early days of the pandemic without also mentioning their streaming content, considering 64 million households watched *Tiger King* in its first month debut and 30 million saw *Love Is Blind*.[1]

Now *that* is a pivot.

Another company that's so enmeshed in our culture is a little $1.7 trillion Japanese brand called Nintendo.

"But wait," you might say, "Nintendo's always been in the electronic toys and games industry."

Except they weren't. Nintendo got its start as a traditional Japanese playing card business, which gels with the idea of eventually moving into electronic gaming. But before then, the company also tried its hand at other industries, including making vacuums and ramen noodles and a short-stay "love hotel."[2] However, they hit their stride when they pivoted to video games and entertainment systems, becoming world renowned for *Donkey Kong* and *Mario Brothers*, which seems a lot more on brand with their origins than a cup of noodles or love shack.

Words of Wisdom

"Pivoting is not the end of the disruption process, but the beginning of the next leg of your journey."

—Jay Samit

One Degree

You may have noticed that I've used "we" far more frequently than "I" when discussing TransPerfect in this book. So often, corporate actions involved not only me but also my business partner, and of course our employees. My goal has been to portray everything fairly and give everyone proper credit, as we were all responsible for building an iconic company.

At TransPerfect's inception, my business partner and I had important things in common. We were both extraordinarily ambitious and inclined to work harder than most people to accomplish our goals. We were both entrepreneurial and motivated to create an entirely new enterprise. And both of us had an enormous amount of perseverance and curiosity.

There's a concept about trajectory that's oft discussed in the aviation industry. Being one degree off. doesn't seem like a big deal in the beginning, because it's such a small amount. But the 1 in 60 rule states that for every one degree that a plane veers off course, it will miss its target destination by 1 mile for every 60 miles flown. The farther you travel, the more off-course you'll be.

For example, if your plane departs LA for Tokyo 1 degree off course, by the time you've flown 6,755 miles, you'll be 112 miles off course.[3] Given enough fuel, it wouldn't be that big a deal to make a circle over the Sea of Japan and land at the proper airport. However, Coach Gary Greenco gives the example of Korean Airliner 007 in 1983. The flight left New York and was headed to Seoul, 1 percent off its intended trajectory. In this case, that 1 percent trajectory put them into Russian airspace, where the jet was summarily shot down and all 269 souls on board perished.[4]

Trajectory matters.

My partner and I were one degree off in our trajectories of how the business should be run. After many years, he and I would come to realize that our goals, aspirations, and values were entirely different, even though we, and our amazing people, had erected a corporate powerhouse that would change the entire landscape in its industry. We'd both evolved over time, and eventually we'd go too many miles to address those initial differences. While that 1 percent wasn't apparent at first, that same difference between us would eventually destroy both our personal relationship and our ability to continue to work together. The worst part was that we had no way to pivot because we didn't set up things right in the beginning.

Learn from my mistake—always bring in an attorney at the outset, no matter how little startup capital you have.

Next Time: A Shareholders' Agreement

Because my business partner and I were 50/50 partners, we had no tiebreaker when it came to input or big decisions. We'd divided 100 shares of common stock between the two of us. Though he had given one of his shares to his mother, there was no circumstance where his mother would vote against him, so the ownership structure invited corporate deadlock.

I believed we needed to have our roles clarified and a formal dispute resolution system in place. When roles aren't defined, there's always disagreement. I liked the idea of bringing in a Board of Directors and he did not, so we found ourselves stuck.

We should have had a shareholders' agreement from day one. This would have helped us align our priorities and vision. A formal shareholders' agreement would have clarified our roles, responsibilities, decision-making, dispute resolution, and what would happen in the event of marriage, divorce, death, and disability. A shareholders' agreement would have given us a clear exit plan when it became apparent that we could no longer run and grow the company together.

We didn't do this in the very beginning because, apart from lacking funds, we were so fixated on the idea of building the premier company in the industry that it didn't occur to us that our dreams would come true and someday we'd no longer be able to work together in that company.

After years of a deterioration in our ability to run the company with one unified voice, the increasing Balkanization of our business, and the challenge of reaching consensus in our boardroom of two on virtually every executive decision, in 2013 I hired attorneys to negotiate a shareholders' agreement. My partner and I could not agree on the terms of it and over the next several months things got much worse.

As heartbreaking and difficult as it was, I determined that the only way to solve our problems was by going to court. I litigated to request that a custodian be put in place to resolve deadlock in the short term and oversee the sale of the company in the longer term. Litigation began in May of 2014.

Just the Facts

Up to 70 percent of business partnerships ultimately fail.[5]

The Beginning of the End/The End of the Beginning

I don't see the value in recounting the dirty laundry that came from the ugly and painful court battle that followed. (But plenty of business reporters did that for me. The details can be found in the court decisions, which are public record.) The horrendous situation that began in 2012 culminated in the worst year of my life in 2014, a time that tested my mettle in ways that I could never have imagined. What was supposed to be my dream company became my worst nightmare.

The litigation continued through August of 2015, when the court's post-trial decision on the merits was issued. Justice prevailed. I was elated. Mission accomplished.

As I had requested in my petition, a custodian was appointed to sell the company in a manner designed to maximize value for all shareholders while maintaining the company as a going concern. The custodian later determined, and the court agreed, that an auction in which both the shareholders and third parties could participate best served these dual objectives. The custodian would serve as a third director until the auction process concluded with regard to matters on which my partner and I could not agree.

Over the next two and a half chaotic years, during which I was confronted with additional and continuous litigation and a host of challenges related to the sale process itself, I continued in my role and focused on growing the company. Thankfully, through the hard work, dedication, and talent of our phenomenal employees, in 2017 we were able to accomplish my longtime dream, that elusive goal that I planned for and fixated on ever since my first day away from Paresco: to be the largest company in the industry. I was ecstatic. We did it!

On February 15, 2018, my 52nd birthday, with the auction process completed, the court decision was affirmed. After 26 years, I would be selling my share of the company. My last day at TransPerfect was in May 2018. My time with TransPerfect was over.

While the bids had been substantially higher during the auction process—during the trial, an expert witness had valued the company at as much as $1.4 billion—shortly before the auction process was over, the combination of a lack of any noncompete agreements and an unexpected series of events that caused bidders to be concerned about the company's ongoing business operations caused the final purchase price offered in the auction to drop precipitously. The end result was that my partner bought me out of my share of the company for approximately $400 million (including cash in the bank).

I walked away with some hard-won knowledge. The first and greatest lesson is that having a shareholders' agreement is a must. Had we done this in the beginning, we'd have saved ourselves years of litigation, enormous legal fees, and so much pain. As a part of this agreement, I recommend insisting on not only customary dispute resolutions, but also an iron-clad noncompete agreement between you and your partner or partners in the event of a sale. In my case, I learned the hard way that if we'd had this in place, I would have most likely cashed out for significantly more money, because bidders would been more comfortable finalizing a higher-value transaction.

Second, I learned that ideally you should have at least 51 percent ownership, assuming you are one of the only two owners. Regardless of the number of owners, try your best to set it up so that you are the ultimate decision-maker. If somehow this proves impossible or it's too late, make sure that you bring on a Board of Directors or Advisors. Not only will they be crucial to end deadlock, but also they often come with a wealth of knowledge, input, and connections.

Third, if you didn't do all this and you see that your partnership is headed for trouble, act as soon as you can. Bring in attorneys who are skilled at handling these matters.

Finally, and to reiterate the lesson Danny Briere mentioned earlier, it's important to periodically take some cash out of the company because you never know what might happen. Had things shaken out differently in court, I might have had far less to show for my 26 years of building TransPerfect.

The Final Pivot

While the end of my TransPerfect tenure wasn't pretty or anticipated, what I thought would be my darkest hour proved to be a complete blessing, a true gift for which I am eternally grateful. I had more than enough time and money to acquire another language solutions company and rebuild it from the ground up, this time doing it entirely my way.

However, I quickly realized I didn't want to do it all over again; I was ready for a complete change.

I'd been given the opportunity to pivot away from what I'd been doing and into what I'd always been too busy to do. For example, I finally got to go on "maternity leave," 15 years after the fact.

After 26 years of being a leader, of being the boss, it turns out that I was ready for the freedom of more time for my family, of being able to travel and not spend the night on the bathroom floor answering emails, of being able to take my sons on college tours and to ballparks around the county, to indulge in more family nights, watching *The Bachelor* and *American Idol* together.

I was finally going to do all those things I'd been having to shelve for years.

Plus, leaving TransPerfect afforded me the opportunity to finally concentrate on the very best Act II, and what I'd always intended to do—pivoting into giving back.

Words of Wisdom

"Every new beginning comes from some other beginning's end."

—Seneca (also Semi-Sonic)

15

Giving

Founding and then selling TransPerfect afforded me the opportunity to create a legacy. While I loved having an impact on helping the world communicate, and it was an important part of my life, it was only one part. It was my Act I. My goal was always to translate that success into something bigger. That's why in Act II, my mission now is to bring the world together by using my resources to achieve equality for everyone in society.

Okay, yes, your first reaction may be that this sounds grandiose and corny. Maybe on some level, it is. But, on the most critical level, with all the good fortune I've had, it's the absolute truth.

Words of Wisdom

"The meaning of life is to find your gift. The purpose of life is to give it away."

—Pablo Picasso

My Second Act

Once the auction was complete, I was excited to set up my next venture—my foundation. This had always been my ultimate plan, as both of my parents had exemplified and instilled in me the importance of service and philanthropy for as long as I can remember.

Right before the end of my time at TransPerfect, I was contacted by a magazine called *Quoted* about "being featured." Several years earlier, amidst the drama and a month before the litigation, I was asked to pose on the cover of *SmartMoney*. It's only natural that I wanted to look my best for the magazine cover, so I was hoping to have my hair and makeup done so I'd present well. On the morning of the *SmartMoney* shoot, I spent four hours locked in battle with my business partner, having a screaming match about the issue du jour. I missed my window to prep for the cover, so when the film crew arrived, I had dirty hair and barely a suggestion of makeup. Seeing that cover reminds me of what a stressful time it was.

So, when *Quoted* contacted me, I had them come to my apartment on my first day away from TransPerfect. I had my hair and makeup done and when I asked them what I should wear, they said I should put on whatever made me happy, so some of the photos show me in a purple sequined gown. The pictorial and interview took up eight pages in the magazine, and we talked about important topics, like my children.

The experience was exhilarating because, as the reporter and I spoke, I came to understand that I was starting an entirely new life and the day felt like a celebration. I realized how excited I was about what I'd do next. Later, when the magazine published, I couldn't believe the contrast between my demeanor in the *Quoted* photos and the accompanying text, versus those in *SmartMoney*; I appeared to be an entirely different person with the monkey of litigation and constant fighting off my back.

As the reporter and I spoke that day, the idea of what was next became more and more clear. The notion of earning more money for the sake of earning money seemed so "yesterday" for me. After a certain threshold—and I understand the inherent privilege that comes from being able to say this—the notion of money *qua* money loses its meaning.

What has meaning to me is figuring out how to help those who haven't had the same opportunities as I have had.

I asked myself, *How can I take the largesse I will never be able to use for myself or my family to take others to another level?*

As I closed the door after the reporter and photographer that day, I plotted my next move, the one that so many ultra-successful businesspeople take once they leave the day-to-day management of their businesses.

I would start a vanity space program and build rocket ships.

Kidding!

With Great Power Comes Great Responsibility

After all was said and done, the big questions I asked myself were: *What do I want to do? Do I want to buy a company? Run a company? Advise on a company? Be on the Board of a Company?*

I had not signed a noncompete, so I was free to work for another language solutions provider, yet I was reticent to get back into that space after three decades.

What I hoped to do was to take all the skills I'd honed and channel them into giving back, a move that plenty of successful businesspeople have done before me. I've been so inspired by what Bill Gates had to say recently when he tweeted, "As I look to the future, I plan to give virtually all of my wealth to the foundation. I will move down and eventually off of the list of the world's richest people,"[1] and "I have an obligation to return my resources to society in ways that have the greatest impact for reducing suffering and improving lives. And I hope others in positions of great wealth and privilege will step up in this moment too."[2]

That's my goal.

I also have such respect for Yvon Chouinard, the founder of Patagonia, who, along with his wife and two children, created a trust to funnel the $3 billion worth of his company into fighting climate change.[3]

While it sounds like charitable giving would be easy—just start writing checks—it's more complicated than at first glance. I can't help but think of that scene from Steve Martin's *The Jerk*, where his suddenly flush character Navin R. Johnson tries to find charitable ventures, from funding a priest trying to prevent cat juggling south of the border, to helping a Texas oilman replace the leather seats on his airplane so he's no longer embarrassed to fly his friends to the Super Bowl.

Being a philanthropist is about much more than simply opening your wallet. It's about giving your time and your expertise to the causes that move you. In fact, consulting organizations now exist to aid the wealthy in how to maximize their charitable giving, such as Bridgespan. Bridgespan advises not only the Bill and Melinda Gates Foundation, but also the Ford and Rockefeller Foundations, as well as nonprofits like the YMCA of the US and the Salvation Army.[4]

Understanding that philanthropy is the ultimate way for unimaginable wealth to benefit society, Warren Buffett, Bill Gates, and Melinda French Gates created the Giving Pledge in 2010. Per the Giving Pledge's website, "The Giving Pledge is a simple concept: an open invitation for billionaires, or those who would be if not for their giving, to publicly commit to give the majority of their wealth to philanthropy either during their lifetimes or in their wills. It is inspired by the example set by millions of people at all income levels who give generously—and often at great personal sacrifice—to make the world better."[5]

For me, figuring out to whom to give was no different from determining what kind of company I wanted to start.

All I had to do was allow my passions to determine what problems I should help solve.

A Solid Foundation

I am where I am today because of entrepreneurship. Entrepreneurship is not only a great equalizer, but it's the key to changing the world, one innovation at a time. So I started the Elizabeth Elting Foundation in early 2018 to advance the equality of women and other marginalized populations. I've seen so many women in the business world experience sexism, and I hated that they were made to feel like the underdog. I started the foundation because I realized how lucky I was to have been born with certain advantages and my mission became to help make those advantages available to others. I firmly believe that everyone deserves to be treated equally, regardless of the situation into which they were born, and this is more important now than ever. No one should ever hear, "Liz! Phone!" shouted across an office full of equals.

TransPerfect bridged the gap with languages, and my intent with the foundation is to bridge gaps in opportunities. The foundation is somewhat of a catchall for my passions; it encompasses everything from creating scholarship opportunities for entrepreneurial young women to funding exciting women-led startups and social businesses, to supporting women-led organizations that foster women's success through educational programs, mentorships, community building, and more. It is primarily about encouraging and developing entrepreneurship as a way of equalizing opportunity. Give a woman a fish and she eats for a day; give her a fishing pole and she feeds herself *and* her community for life.

Thanks to Raghu Sundaram, Amanda Parker, and Deepak Hegde, one of my foundation's entrepreneur-based ventures is to support the Endless Frontier Labs at NYU's Stern School of Business. Endless Frontier Labs is an accelerator program that guides founders through a performance-based mentoring process. It is thrilling to be a part of EFL because it's open to early-stage life science and technology startups, allowing founders from around the world to make connections in the thriving New York startup ecosystem and US markets. The companies I help fund could literally help cure cancer.

My foundation provides funding for numerous and varied promising ventures featuring women in leadership positions or women-centric businesses that have successfully completed the program. What's exciting about the EFL is that its mission mirrors the goals and drive behind the Elizabeth Elting Foundation, and I'm grateful to partner with NYU to support women-led startups with the potential to change the world. These companies deserve recognition for their industriousness, clarity of vision, and purity of purpose, and getting to be a small part of their future triumphs, here at the ground floor, is a true honor. The ambition and sophistication of each and every Elizabeth Elting Venture Fund recipient blows me away, and I count myself fortunate to be able to support their visions.

Under the umbrella of entrepreneurship, I'm delighted to help support BasBlue, a Detroit club where women are able to congregate for networking, curated programming, meetups, fireside chats, and educational seminars, with meeting rooms and collaboration spaces. It's a launching pad for big ideas.

In the world of social impact entrepreneurship, thanks to Nancy Brown, Greg Mandell, and Meg Gilmartin, I've teamed up with the American Heart Association to create the Elizabeth Elting Social Impact Fund to support the mission of addressing inequities in marginalized communities, so *everyone* can live longer, healthier lives.

What I love about this program is that it merges better health with entrepreneurship. Social impact entrepreneurs apply for Social Impact Fund grants to address the connections between personal health and its social determinants, such as housing, employment, nutrition security, and mental health. The fund supports local entrepreneurs, small businesses, and organizations that are breaking down social and economic barriers to healthy lives. The AHA selects the recipients, who are often women of color, and then I help fund these social entrepreneurs.

On a global level, I'm involved in Elluminate, a group that supports women entrepreneurs around the world who are addressing a variety of human rights issues. In addition, I frequently speak about entrepreneurship because I love sharing what I've learned. When I'm not in front of young minds, I share my knowledge and experience with columns in both *Forbes* and *Swaay*.

Supporting entrepreneurs is one of my greatest passions because entrepreneurs change the world and being an entrepreneur is something anyone can do. The notion of helping others build their dream and create their own ideal corporate culture will always be a draw for me.

Another one of my passions is supporting education. Like entrepreneurship, education is another great equalizer and a path out of poverty and diminished circumstances. Through education, we learn to think and it's how we grow and connect through shared understanding. That's why I now serve on the Board of Trustees at Trinity College, where I have the good fortune to work with Joanne Berger-Sweeney, Sonia Cardenas, and their terrific team. I also serve on NYU Stern's Board of Overseers and fund a number of scholarships for women MBAs at NYU Stern each year.

An educational cause that is near and dear to my heart and which I'm on the board of is GLAM—Girls Learning Advanced Math. I got involved because of a young girl named Tessa Wayne, who went to school with my sons. She noticed as she got into the more advanced math classes, fewer and fewer girls participated, so she created a mentorship program for younger female learners to provide them with math enrichment and to simply have fun with math. She started in New York, and now has branches in Boston, New Haven, and Palo

Alto, where she is attending college. What's so meaningful is that GLAM focuses on encouraging girls to stay in math and to seriously consider having careers in STEM. The feedback I've heard from the young women in the group is that through GLAM mentorship, they're much more confident in math and that has already had a meaningful impact on their career plans and their lives.

Another way I support women is by working with NOW, the National Organization for Women, helping push forward women's rights on all issues that impact women, from abortion rights access to human trafficking to equal pay. I'm also a founding sponsor of Lift Our Voices. Following their own experiences, Gretchen Carlson and Julie Roginsky created this nonprofit to eradicate the silencing of survivors of workplace abuse and to promote awareness for workers so they understand their rights related to all forms of misconduct to create an inclusive, respectful, and safe workplace for all.

Closely related to the goals of my foundation, I'm also very interested in improving the quality and duration of lives, so healthcare is another area of foundation activity. I'm active in BCRF, the Breast Cancer Research Foundation—the highest-rated breast cancer organization in the country—because breast cancer is the number one diagnosed cancer in women. In 2017, I founded the Elting Family Research Fund to support initiatives for the International Waldenstrom's Macroglobulinemia Foundation. This is a cause that's particularly close to my heart as Waldenstrom is a type of lymphoma that my father has been fighting for 12 years now. . .after he was given 3 to 5 years to live. Thanks to the IWMF, not only has the life expectancy been raised to 18 to 20 years, but it's also helping those battling leukemia, which my uncle has been fighting for a number of years. In addition, I support Gabrielle's Angel Foundation, which funds research to prevent, detect, treat, and ultimately eradicate lymphoma and leukemia.

I'm also on the American Heart Association's GRFW National Leadership Council. Heart disease is the number one killer of women (and men). Our goals are to reduce death and disability from heart disease and stroke and help everyone live longer, healthier lives.

Another issue that I find critical in today's society is addressing gun safety. I'm alarmed that in a country with 4 percent of the global population, we own 42 percent of the guns, and have exponentially more mass shootings, suicides, and gun violence than any other first world country. That's why I work with Everytown for Gun Safety, which was founded by Michael Bloomberg as Mayors Against Illegal Guns. It is nonpartisan, with more than 2,000 current and former mayors and has a grassroots network, Moms Demand Action, with over 10 million supporters. As the largest gun safety organization in the country, it is fighting to get the right candidates elected, advance gun safety in the courts, enact smart gun policies, and demand accountability, all in order to end gun violence.

In addition, I'm part of Sandy Hook Promise's Inaugural Leadership Council, and Board of Advisors which is also nonpartisan, and I participate in donating and fundraising. SHP trains students and staff in schools and provides crisis centers to identify and prevent mass shootings and suicides, as well as helps draft legislation to get gun safety bills put into law.

I'm active in The Campaign Against Hunger, and my foundation provided more than 100,000 meals last year. While working for a changed future is so important, we can't lose sight of the fact that too many people are hungry right now.

When I was running TransPerfect, I tried to create the ideal corporate culture. I loved the idea of diverse people coming together, so at every event I tried to seat everyone in groups who didn't know each other or didn't normally interact. I saw such value in everyone mingling, talking, and sharing ideas, rather than just sticking with their own buddies at a table in the corner. In a way, I'm trying to do this with my philanthropy work, too. I'm merging circles, making introductions, cross-pollinating. And I believe bringing people together to listen to and learn from one another is critical to how we begin to solve what appear to be intractable challenges in our country and the world as a whole.

My children always ask me, "Why don't you just sleep in one day?" But the more I started doing, the more I realized there was for me to do. I'm as busy now as I was back in the TransPerfect days. I'm still sitting down every December and plotting out my goals for the coming new year; none of that has changed, save for my purpose. At some point, I should likely hone in on a few causes and put all my efforts into those, but I believe in everything currently on my plate. Every morning

I wake up and wonder, "What problem can I help solve?" so you can see my reticence about sleeping in.

I feel incredibly blessed to be able to leverage my corporate experience, from sales and marketing, to operations, to wrangling the legal system, to put forth good in the world, particularly for women and those who haven't had my advantages.

I used my resources to win big, building my dream company. Now I'm using them to build my dream world, and I couldn't be more excited to make this my legacy.

Because now more than ever, I understand that if it's to be, it's up to me.

Liz's Life Lesson

Never forget that you are your own greatest resource. When you work harder than most, the world is there for the taking. . .and then, the changing.

Notes

Chapter 1

1. www.bloomberg.com/news/articles/2021-09-23/female-mba-grads-earn-11-000-less-than-male-peers-study-finds
2. www.forbes.com/sites/ashleystahl/2022/01/21/the-pandemic-and-the-gender-pay-gap-in-2022/?sh=3f46ea87347d
3. www.forbes.com/sites/forbesbusinesscouncil/2021/09/21/overcoming-some-of-the-barriers-to-women-entrepreneurship/?sh=31084d327800

Chapter 2

1. www.forbes.com/sites/jessicamendoza1/2019/04/10/living-abroad-boosts-your-decision-making-clarity/?sh=5cdf0a085eff
2. knowablemagazine.org/article/mind/2018/how-second-language-can-boost-brain
3. tessais.org/children-learn-languages-faster-adults/#:~:text=Later%20in%20life%2C%20those%20neural,languages%20at%20a%20faster%20rate
4. www.forbes.com/sites/theyec/2020/12/16/why-following-your-passion-is-not-enough-to-be-successful/?sh=61c78d2a6411
5. www.businessinsider.com/great-company-names-2018-5
6. www.opinionx.co/99-problems
7. freakonomics.com/podcast/extra-mark-zuckerberg-full-interview/
8. www.sfgate.com/food/article/Concierge-grocery-shopping-4340149.php
9. www.youtube.com/watch?v=wkmR7TYUt_c

Chapter 3

1. https://www.entrepreneur.com/growing-a-business/fred-smith/197542
2. minutes.co/82-of-small-businesses-fail-because-of-cash-flow-problems-here-are-3-ways-to-fix-that/
3. www.dcwgrp.com/blog/how-amazon-took-down-toysrus-and-what-it-means-for-your-benefit-plan
4. slidebean.com/story/first-kodak-digital-camera
5. www.businessinsider.com/xerox-was-actually-first-to-invent-the-pc-they-just-forgot-to-do-anything-with-it-2012-2
6. slate.com/business/2013/01/zipcar-bought-by-avid-budget-group-for-500-million.html
7. bettermarketing.pub/how-yahoo-missed-out-on-hundreds-of-billions-again-and-again-905f3bc86413

Chapter 4

1. www.forbes.com/sites/annabelacton/2017/11/03/how-to-set-goals-and-why-you-should-do-it/?sh=3af84328162d
2. www.washingtonpost.com/local/education/half-the-world-is-bilingual-whats-our-problem/2019/04/24/1c2b0cc2-6625-11e9-a1b6-b29b90efa879_story.html
3. observer.com/2017/03/psychological-secrets-hack-better-life-habits-psychology-productivity/#:~:text=The%20American%20Society%20of%20Training,success%20by%20up%20to%2095%25
4. hbr.org/2020/11/how-apple-is-organized-for-innovation
5. clutchpoints.com/michael-phelps-net-worth-in-2022

Chapter 5

1. www.c2fo.com/amer/us/en-us/resource-center/article/04282021/6-companies-that-faced-adversity-and-came-back-stronger
2. www.theguardian.com/lifeandstyle/2017/jun/04/how-lego-clicked-the-super-brand-that-reinvented-itself
3. www.licenseglobal.com/trends-insights/almost-bankrupt-most-profitable-toy-company-lessons-lego

4. www.entrepreneur.com/leadership/6-principles-for-overcoming-entrepreneurial-adversity/275571

5. www.entrepreneur.com/growing-a-business/5-companies-that-grew-too-quickly-and-what-you-can-learn/310166

6. www.cbsnews.com/news/my-company-grew-too-fast-and-went-out-of-business/

7. www.verywellmind.com/unbelievable-facts-about-optimists-1717551

Chapter 6

1. www.forbes.com/sites/micahsolomon/2015/01/15/the-amazing-true-story-of-the-hotel-that-saved-thomas-the-tank-engine/?sh=42927c54230e

2. haiilo.com/blog/employee-engagement-8-statistics-you-need-to-know/

3. www.huffpost.com/entry/how-empowering-your-employees-helps-improve-business_b_5a2eec0ee4b0bad787126f08

4. www.entrepreneur.com/business-news/that-act-of-kindness-meant-so-much-chewys-customer/429689

5. www.linkedin.com/pulse/building-innovation-cultureapple-james-browning

Chapter 7

1. www.nytimes.com/2021/07/24/sports/olympics/gymnastics-balance-beam.html#:~:text=Overview,of%20a%20coronavirus%20vaccination%20card

2. www.usatoday.com/story/opinion/voices/2019/11/22/motherhood-child-care-women-bias-workplace-discrimination-column/4261758002/

3. www.nytimes.com/2014/09/07/upshot/a-child-helps-your-career-if-youre-a-man.html

4. hbswk.hbs.edu/item/kids-benefit-from-having-a-working-mom

5. www.forbes.com/sites/lizelting/2021/03/08/women-have-lost-more-than-jobs-in-this-pandemic/?sh=3a9a66164c5d

6. www.cnbc.com/2020/10/07/elizabeth-eltings-career-tips-for-women-during-the-pandemic.html

7. hbr.org/2018/09/do-longer-maternity-leaves-hurt-womens-careers

8. news.yahoo.com/maternity-leave-stigma-undermining-womens-careers-050055542.html

9. www.thepennyhoarder.com/make-money/career/companies-paid-maternity-leave/

10. innovation.mit.edu/news-article/the-guardian-i-cant-remember-feeling-as-excited-about-the-future-redesigning-space-travel-for-women/

11. www.forbes.com/sites/lizelting/2022/07/22/in-dialogue-diva-founder-and-ceo-carinne-chambers-saiani-on-entrepreneurship-and-fighting-for-womens-rights/?sh=2e8a4fb51afa

Chapter 8

1. www.businessinsider.com/uber-vs-lyft-biggest-differences-a-researcher-found-in-5000-miles-alex-rosenblatt-uberland-book-2018-10

2. www.cnbc.com/2019/04/13/uber-is-way-more-complicated-than-lyft-and-investors-shouldnt-value-them-the-same-way.html

3. startuptalky.com/coca-cola-pepsi-business-model/

4. www.investopedia.com/articles/markets/081415/comparing-cocacola-and-pepsis-business-models.asp

5. backlinko.com/amazon-prime-users

6. www.businesswire.com/news/home/20210616005050/en/New-Research-Finds-65-of-Consumers-Willing-to-Pay-More-for-Faster-Deliveries

7. retailwire.com/discussion/can-in-store-coffee-add-pep-to-retail-sales/

8. www.zippia.com/advice/career-change-statistics/#:~:text=How%20often%20do%20successful%20people,the%20highest%20rates%20of%20success

9. www.mylanguageconnection.com/translation-industry-trends-and-statistics/#:~:text=Translation%20Industry%20Statistics,America%20follows%20this%20at%2039.41%25

Chapter 9

1. www.failory.com/blog/startup-failure-rate

2. sujanpatel.com/business/7-lessons-from-5-failed-companies/

3. www.washingtonpost.com/news/morning-mix/wp/2014/07/08/crumbs-the-cupcakery-that-couldnt-goes-broke/

4. As of November 2022, Crumbs is staging a national relaunch. I'll be interested to see what they do differently this time. Per their website, they're looking into supermarket placement, delivery, and wholesale orders, so it sounds like they've learned from history. Whether they'll sell green juice too is yet to be announced.

5. www.bankrate.com/finance/credit-cards/history-of-women-and-credit-cards/

6. thriveglobal.com/stories/why-its-time-for-women-to-break-the-money-taboo/

7. www.forbes.com/sites/nextavenue/2018/06/24/6-ways-women-can-overcome-the-money-taboo/?sh=2a2371147372

8. www.psychologytoday.com/us/blog/the-human-side-finance/201807/the-common-misconceptions-about-wealthy-upbringing

Chapter 10

1. Unless you have celiac disease, in which case I am sorry.

2. www.pbs.org/newshour/health/tylenol-murders-1982#:~:text=McNeil%20Consumer%20Products%2C%20a%20subsidiary,bottles%20of%20Tylenol%20in%20circulation

3. www.nytimes.com/2002/03/23/your-money/IHT-tylenol-made-a-hero-of-johnson-johnson-the-recall-that-started.html

4. www.businessinsider.com/toyota-paying-billions-because-of-marketing-failures-2012-12

5. www.avihein.com/2010/03/30/toyota-example-of-a-crisis-communications-fail/

6. www.npr.org/2013/09/20/224296660/why-companies-and-ceos-rarely-admit-to-wrongdoing

7. www.inc.com/ken-sterling/why-taking-ownership-of-your-errors-improves-work-culture-leadership.html

8. www.nytimes.com/2017/10/08/business/dove-ad-racist.html

9. www.newyorker.com/tech/annals-of-technology/e-mail-is-making-us-miserable

10. www.inc.com/geoffrey-james/new-study-the-average-worker-spends-30-hours-a-week-checking-email.html

11. www.shrm.org/resourcesandtools/hr-topics/organizational-and-employee-development/pages/the-cost-of-poor-communication.aspx

12. medium.com/@Jude.M/how-great-leaders-communicate-big-vision-so-that-others-want-to-join-in-d3296e7ca37e

Chapter 11

1. www.lifehack.org/287785/10-differences-between-boss-and-real-leader
2. www.forbes.com/sites/lizelting/2019/11/22/the-twilight-of-integrity/?sh=4f322c997c67
3. www.fastcompany.com/3034164/muppet-performers-share-what-it-was-like-to-work-for-jim-henson#:~:text=Far%20from%20lazy%2C%20he%20worked,time%20and%20space%20to%20create
4. www.forbes.com/sites/michaelbarthur/2020/03/06/remembering-jack-welch--and-his-legacy-over-your-career/?sh=5eb325714d28
5. www.inc.com/jason-aten/how-amazons-departing-ceo-jeff-bezos-prioritizes-his-time-according-to-one-way-door-rule.html
6. www.worldvision.org/disaster-relief-news-stories/2012-hurricane-sandy-facts
7. home.treasury.gov/system/files/271/Q2.21-ICIC-Recession-Recovery-Tracker-Report-Draft-Formatted-with-Cover-11.3.21.pdf
8. startupbonsai.com/covid19-and-small-businesses-statistics/
9. time.com/6082576/pandemic-new-businesses/
10. www.qualtrics.com/blog/workplace-culture-innovation/#:~:text=Companies%20with%20a%20"highly%20aligned,itself%20up%20for%20greater%20success
11. www.businessinsider.com/how-employers-can-use-googles-20-rule-boost-workers-creativity-2020-8
12. rework.withgoogle.com/blog/new-re-work-guides-on-innovation/

Chapter 12

1. www.shrm.org/resourcesandtools/hr-topics/talent-acquisition/pages/the-real-costs-of-recruitment.aspx
2. www.gsb.stanford.edu/insights/meg-whitman-how-we-grew-ebay-30-13000-employees
3. www.forbes.com/sites/michaeltnietzel/2022/03/04/amazon-expands-its-free-college-tuition-program-to-140-colleges-and-universities/?sh=484df09d2eb6
4. ripplematch.com/career-advice/companies-that-offer-exceptional-professional-development-programs-for-entry-level-employees-f53abebf/
5. snacknation.com/blog/employee-engagement-companies/

6. www.tinypulse.com/blog/employee-retention-examples

7. www.tinypulse.com/blog/employee-retention-examples

8. www.loreal.com/-/media/project/loreal/brand-sites/corp/master/lcorp/press-releases/hr-and-diversity/loral-launches-fit-culture-app-a-custommade-app-to-welcome-new-employees/tt3ntc1214pz-1-201.pdf?rev=3c6cc5d3dfcd4245ab992f62d382bcde

9. www.cnbc.com/2022/05/10/-the-great-resignation-has-changed-the-workplace-for-good-.html

10. www.forbes.com/sites/forbescoachescouncil/2019/04/01/are-your-employees-engaged-at-work/?sh=6be6c25215c8

11. hbr.org/2014/10/the-value-of-keeping-the-right-customers#:~:text=Depending%20on%20which%20study%20you,than%20retaining%20an%20existing%20one

Chapter 13

1. www.linkedin.com/business/talent/blog/talent-acquisition/crucial-hiring-lesson-that-sheryl-sandberg-learned-from-meg-whitman

2. www.zippia.com/advice/recruitment-statistics/

3. www.forbes.com/sites/susanadams/2012/04/05/why-promoting-from-within-usually-beats-hiring-from-outside/?sh=3380f53636ce

4. diversity-inclusion-speakers.com/news/tips-and-tricks/benefits-diversity-inclusion-workplace-statistics/

5. hbr.org/2013/12/how-diversity-can-drive-innovation

6. www.peoplemanagement.co.uk/article/1742040/diversity-drives-better-decisions

7. www.glassdoor.com/employers/blog/diversity/

8. rockcontent.com/blog/brand-purpose-diversity/

9. www.forbes.com/sites/lizelting/2022/09/22/stop-saying-quotas-dont-work-because-they-demonstrably-do/?sh=216ca11e5b9c

Chapter 14

1. variety.com/2020/tv/news/netflix-tiger-king-love-is-blind-viewing-64-million-1234586272/

2. www.theceomagazine.com/business/marketing/famous-and-successful-business-pivots/

3. www.linkedin.com/pulse/difference-1-degree-change-makes-randell-turner-ph-d-/
4. www.garygreeno.com/one-degree-can-make-all-the-difference/
5. www.forbes.com/sites/allbusiness/2019/03/13/keep-business-partnership-from-imploding/?sh=1eaeafc27338

Chapter 15

1. twitter.com/BillGates/status/1547235392721629185?ref_src=twsrc%5Etfw%7Ctwcamp%5Etweetembed%7Ctwterm%5E1547235395078803457%7Ctwgr%5Eba3fcef0ec6e280d1bc0d4945b5e3e53e756cdf7%7Ctwcon%5Es2_&ref_url=https%3A%2F%2Fwww.cnbc.com%2F2022%2F07%2F15%2Fbill-gates-plans-to-give-away-virtually-all-his-113-billion-fortune.html
2. twitter.com/BillGates/status/1547235395078803457
3. www.nytimes.com/2022/09/14/climate/patagonia-climate-philanthropy-chouinard.html
4. www.nytimes.com/2021/11/15/business/billionaires-donating-consulting.html
5. givingpledge.org/about

Acknowledgments

How fortunate I feel not only to have lived my dream of building a billion-dollar business, but now to be able to add the title of author to the list of those realized dreams. Much like with my company, I didn't reach this milestone alone, so I want to extend my eternal thanks.

First, thank you so much to my husband, Mike—your encouragement and patience over the last 35 years have been such a blessing. You're the best sounding board and an endless source of big ideas. Together we are better, and I can never thank you enough.

For my sons, Jay and Zack—thank you for giving me the best job I've ever had, which is being your mother. I continually learn so much from you both and I couldn't be prouder of the men you've become.

For my parents—you made me who I am today. Your collective boundless enthusiasm, creativity, and lust for life taught me that the world was big and beautiful. The confidence you helped instill by having me forge my own path has enabled me to pursue my dreams and I'll always be grateful. How lucky I am to have you as my parents!

For Lynn Elting Siegel, my dear sister, and Joanne Elting, thank you for being there for me, and all the years of joy and happy memories. And many thanks and much love to Rob, Lucy, Molly (not the cat), and Cody Siegel, and Diana, Jack, Sharona, and Joel Kahn. For Eric and Lisa Elting, Heather and Kurt Elting-Ballard, Peter and Wes Elting, and Richard, Mindy (RIP), Bob, Sandy, and Louise (RIP) Chapman, all my love and gratitude.

For those who've been a part of the publishing process, including my editors Victoria Savanh, Michelle Hacker, Amy Handy, Sharmila Srinivasan, and Kim Wimpsett, thank you for giving me the opportunity to share what I've learned. It's been such an honor being a part of the Wiley family, and I'd like to extend my thanks to everyone who makes books happen, from art direction to production to sales to marketing to publicity. I so appreciate what you do. And for Erin Niumata at Folio Lit and everyone at BookHighlight, including Polly Floyd, Alana Whitman, and Margaret Wiggins, thank you for your guidance and keen insight. Thanks to Mark Fortier, Chandler Kuck, and Emma van Bergen.

For Jen Lancaster, my collaborator, thanks for your brilliance, humor, enthusiasm, and patience in helping me hone my story. You are the absolute best, one in a million! What a fun journey this has been!

For those skilled advisors who helped me attain lift, not only getting this book off the ground but all the way to the finish line, I want to extend all my gratitude to Mark Segall, Eric Yaverbaum, Devan Gallagher, Magdalene Visales, Tessa Freeman, Juliana Rowane, Fatou Bah, and Diana Lee. And for my mentor, Jack Daly, who did the same with this guidance on my career and professional life. All my thanks go to Phil Kaufman, Ron Greenberg, Eric Rayman, and Danny Briere for your insight.

I owe so much of my success to those who helped build my dream, creating not only a world-class company but also a second family. You forever have my respect and admiration, Sylvia Ananicz, Ken Anders, Gale Boodram, Alicja Borek, George Buelna, Colleen Chulis, Bob DeNoia (RIP), Ben Harrison, Anne Hoehn, Jennifer LeCates, Kelly Marek, Kerri Malmgren, Marco Marino, Matt Mores, Mark Peeler, Thomas Pennell, Maria Simon, Connie Suneborn, and Jamie Wengroff as well as my other colleagues, the thousands of employees who built TransPerfect, and who I consider friends and was blessed to work with over the years. I'm so proud of and grateful for all of you.

Many thanks to my brilliant photographer, Melanie Dunea. (This was way better than that *SmartMoney* shoot, FYI.)

Because it takes a village, I want to extend my deepest thanks to Bibi Jadunath, who has been with us for over 22 years, since Zack was born, and is family. We all love you.

I also want to recognize my loving, supportive friends from all stages of my life. They supported me through life. You all are why I've never had a therapist, because God knows I need one. (And extra special thanks to the few who endured too many book-related conversations.)

From my childhood, thank you to my *Charlie's Angels* partner in crime-solving, Steffi Black, as well as Eta Rottenberg and Amy Swidler. Also, many thanks to my college and B-school friends, including Penni Berns, Liz Brine, Leslie DeCillis, Amy Goldenberg, Suzanna Keith, Beth McDonald, Cathy Nemser, Laura Poppiti, Jill Robbins, and Karen Rubin. Thanks for keeping me fun! The same goes for Mona Andrews, Galit Ben-Joseph, Johanna Berkman, Valerie Bowling, Cristina Civetta, Cori Cohen, Pam Dickstein, Sanjyot Dunung, Pam Esterson, Mela Garber, Erika Greff, Wendy Holmes, Kirsten Jordan, Sonia Kapoor, Liz Ketels, Lori Levinson, Sonia Ossorio, Elise Perlmutter, Bobbi Rebell, Kristine Reynal, David Sher, Isabelle Silverman, Leah Silverman, Sharon Singer, Julie Teitel, Debby Tukel, Judy Turchin, Rosanne Vinson, Marla Wasserman, Shari Wayne, and Rachel Weinstein.

I'm so appreciative to those who helped with the title/content/ cover brainstorming sessions, so a million thanks to Carolyn and Rich Amsinger, Kim Azzarelli, Dianne Bailey, Peter Barcia, Estelle Erasmus, Gloria Feldt, Lydia Fenet, Elizabeth Haney, Carla Harris, Deepak Hegde, Joan and George Hornig, Susan Jurevics, Jill Kargman, Michele Keene, Karthik Krishnan, Aliza Licht, Beth Murray, Candace Nelson, Iman Oubou, Amanda Parker, Michele Rella, Denise Rich, Kim Rittberg, Jeff Saeger, Melania Schnollbegun, Joan Schwartzberg, and Don Weiss. I have much gratitude for your efforts. Dinner is on me.

Tremendous gratitude for all those who took the time to read and endorse this work. I am eternally grateful to Arianna Huffington, Sheryl Sandberg, Joanne Berger-Sweeney, Michael Bloomberg, Gretchen Carlson, Billie Jean King, Danny Meyer, Scott Galloway, Jack Daly, Danny Briere, Tina Brown, Gloria Steinem, and Raghu Sundaram. All I can say is, wow.

For Daisy Kudish, Jerry Mryglot, and Tom Clark, and all of the incredibly talented linguists for whom I have the utmost respect— without you, there would be no TransPerfect. For everyone I had the privilege to call my employees or my clients during the TransPerfect days, thank you so much for allowing me the opportunity to prove myself, back in the days when you dropped by the dorm room unexpectedly. I appreciate your faith in me more than you will ever know.

Finally, for those of you with big ideas, the entrepreneurs who have what it takes to translate their own passions into purpose: thank you so much for reading. Remember, when you build your dreams, you always win.

About the Author

Liz Elting, founder and CEO of the Elizabeth Elting Foundation, is a New York–based philanthropist and businesswoman, recognized for her outstanding entrepreneurship and focus on developing women business leaders. These recognitions and awards include the *Working Woman* Entrepreneurial Excellence Award for Customer Service, the Ernst and Young Entrepreneur of the Year Award, the American Express *Entrepreneur* magazine Woman of the Year Award, the Distinguished Alumnae Award from NYU Stern's Women in Business, the Women Worth Watching Award from *Diversity Journal*, the Trinity College Alumni Medal for Excellence and Gary McQuaid Award, the *Enterprising Women* magazine Enterprising Women of the Year Award, the National Organization for Women's Women of Power & Influence Award, the 2019 Charles Waldo Haskins Award for business and public service from NYU's Stern School of Business, the American Heart Association's 2020 Health Equity Leadership Award, and the Alliance of Women Entrepreneurs' 2021 Vertex Award for changing the face and direction of women's high-growth entrepreneurship. In 2022, Elting was honored with the American Heart Association's Woman Changing the World Award, Trinity College's Kathleen O'Connor Boelhouwer '85 Alumni Initiative Award, and was an honoree at the 25th Anniversary Celebration of the Jewish Women's Foundation of New York. In addition, Elting has been named one of *Forbes'* Richest Self-Made Women every year since the list's inception.

An accomplished business leader, Elting cofounded TransPerfect, the world's largest provider of language and business solutions. Headquartered in New York City, the company has over $1.1 billion in revenue and more than 7,000 employees in over 100 cities around the globe.

Elting has been profiled in a number of books, including *American Dream: Interviews with Industry-Leading Professionals* by Jason Navallo, the *New York Times* bestseller *Succeed by Your Own Terms* (McGraw-Hill), *Leadership Secrets of the World's Most Successful CEOs* (Dearborn Trade Publishing), and *Straight Talk About Starting and Growing Your Business* (McGraw-Hill). She is featured regularly in the media, including the *New York Times*, the *Wall Street Journal*, *Forbes*, *O*, *Oprah* magazine, the *Financial Times*, *Reader's Digest*, *Huffington Post*, and *Crain's New York Business*.

During Elting's time as co-CEO, TransPerfect was an eight-time winner of the Inc. 5000 Award, alongside winning the 2015 SmartCEO Corporate Culture Awards, and was named the Internet Marketing Association's Best Translation Solution at the IMPACT15 Conference, among numerous other accolades.

Elting serves on the NYU Stern School of Business Board of Directors, the Trinity College Board of Trustees, is a founding member of Trinity's Women's Leadership Council and the Marjorie Butcher Circle, and is a regular speaker at both NYU and Columbia Business Schools. Elting also serves on the American Heart Association's Go Red for Women National Leadership Council, the Sandy Hook Promise Inaugural Leadership Council, and Board of Advisors and the Board of Directors of Girls Learning Advanced Math (GLAM). In 2017, she founded the Elting Family Research Fund to support initiatives for the International Waldenstrom's Macroglobulinemia Foundation.

Elting holds an MBA in finance and international business from the Stern School of Business at New York University and a BA in modern languages and literatures from Trinity College in Hartford, Connecticut.

Through Elting's endeavors, she continues to work to connect the world.

Index